Hurry-Up
PASTA
RECIPES

Publications International, Ltd.

ISBN: 1-56173-968-5

Pictured on front cover: Pasta Delight *(page 76)*.

Pictured on back cover (top to bottom): Southwest Ruffle Salad *(page 6)*, Zesty Artichoke Basil Sauce *(page 92)* and Ham Pasta Primavera *(page 43)*.

8   7   6   5   4   3   2   1

Manufactured in U.S.A.

Microwave ovens vary in wattage and power output; cooking times given with microwave directions in this publication may need to be adjusted. Consult manufacturer's instructions for suitable microwave-safe cooking dishes.

Butter Flavor Crisco® is artificially flavored.

This edition published by Publications International, Ltd. 7373 N. Cicero Ave., Lincolnwood, IL 60646.

Hurry-Up PASTA RECIPES

Pasta popularity is at an all-time high and for good reason, too! This nearly perfect food of milled wheats and water is economical, nutritious and versatile. To discover some of pasta's colorful history and origins, be sure to read Pasta Facts. Time-Saving Tips and Helpful How-To's show you how pasta is a natural convenience food and will give both the seasoned chef and eager novice guidelines for cooking success.

PASTA FACTS

• Noodles originated in Germany in the 13th century. They derive their name from the German word "Nudel," which means a pasta product made with eggs and shaped into ribbons.

• Pasta is a great source of complex carbohydrates. It also contains six essential amino acids, three B-complex vitamins and iron.

• It is from the durum and other hard wheats that pasta receives its yellow amber color, nutty flavor and ability to retain its shape and firmness when cooked.

• Ingredients are added to give pasta a variety of colors. Beets and tomatoes give a reddish hue, carrots an orange tint, spinach a green tone and squid ink a black shade.

• Pasta is available in more than 150 different shapes! Most pasta products can be classified as either long goods (spaghetti), short goods (macaroni), specialty products (shells and bow ties) or egg noodles (pasta made with eggs). Egg noodles contain some cholesterol while non-egg pastas are cholesterol free.

• Pasta in its dry, uncooked form can be stored almost indefinitely in a cool dry place. Fresh pasta will last several weeks in the refrigerator or can also be frozen for up to one month.

• Each year Americans eat more than 4 billion pounds of pasta. That comes to more than 17 pounds per person. In comparison, Italy averages 55 pounds of pasta per person per year.

TIME-SAVING TIPS

• Plan on preparing an extra batch of your favorite pasta soup. Simply pour into serving-size freezer containers and freeze. Thaw and reheat for a last-minute dinner or heartwarming lunch. Extra pasta sauce can also be frozen for later use.

• Lasagna, manicotti and stuffed shells are perfect dishes to prepare and then freeze for another time. Try freezing these casseroles in single-serving portions for days when everyone is eating at different times. Simply cook in the microwave or conventional oven.

• When heating up that big pot of water, plan on cooking more pasta than you'll need. Plain leftover pasta is a great addition to salads, soups, side dishes and casseroles. Simply store the extra pasta in a plastic bag in the refrigerator where it will keep for several days. Freshen the pasta by rinsing with hot or cold water, depending on how you plan to use it. Extra pasta can also be frozen, and then reheated in boiling water or microwaved for a fresh-cooked texture and taste.

• Combine leftover cooked meats, poultry, fish and vegetables with your favorite pasta shape and a simple sauce for a fast and exciting new meal.

HELPFUL HOW-TO'S

Peeling Garlic Cloves

Microwave Method: To quickly peel whole garlic cloves, place the desired number of cloves in a small glass custard cup. Microwave at HIGH (100% power) until slightly softened, 5 to 10 seconds for 1 clove or 45 to 55 seconds for a whole head. Then just slip the garlic out of its skin; nothing could be easier!

Conventional Method: To peel whole garlic cloves, trim off the ends and drop cloves into boiling water for 5 to 10 seconds. Immediately plunge into cold water, then drain. The peels should slip right off. If the cloves are to be minced there is no need to boil them. Simply trim off the ends and crush with the bottom of a heavy saucepan or the flat side of a large knife. The peels can then be easily removed.

Cooking Pasta

• For every pound of dry pasta, bring 4 to 6 quarts of water to a full rolling boil. Add two teaspoons salt, if desired. Gradually add the pasta, allowing the water to return to a boil. The boiling water helps circulate the pasta so that it cooks more evenly. Stir frequently to prevent the pasta from sticking to the pot. Begin testing for doneness after 5 minutes of cooking. Pasta that is "al dente" — meaning "to the tooth" — is tender yet firm. Draining the pasta as soon as it is done will stop the cooking action and help prevent over-cooked pasta. Rinsing is necessary only if the recipe specifies to do so. For best results, serve the pasta within minutes of leaving the pot.

• Add a pinch of your favorite herb or spice directly to pasta cooking water, or add a little lemon or lime juice for flavor in place of salt.

• If pasta is to be used in a dish that requires further cooking, such as a casserole, undercook it slightly.

Easy Equivalents

• In general, 4 ounces of cheese will equal 1 cup shredded cheese. Cheese will shred and grate easier if it is cold.

• Two whole chicken breasts (about 10 ounces each) will yield about 2½ cups chopped cooked chicken.

• One cup of uncooked macaroni-type pasta (including twists and tubes such as rotini and mostaccioli) will yield 2 cups cooked pasta. For egg noodles, 1 cup uncooked will equal 1¼ cups cooked.

Southwest Ruffle Salad

⅔ cup HELLMANN'S® or BEST
  FOODS® Real Mayonnaise
⅓ cup sour cream
¼ cup chopped cilantro
2 tablespoons milk
2 tablespoons lime juice
1 fresh jalapeno pepper,
  seeded and minced
1 teaspoon salt
7 ounces MUELLER'S® Pasta
  Ruffles, cooked, rinsed with
  cold water and drained
2 large tomatoes, seeded and
  chopped
1 yellow bell pepper, chopped
1 zucchini, quartered
  lengthwise and thinly
  sliced
3 green onions, thinly sliced

In large bowl, combine
mayonnaise, sour cream, cilantro,
milk, lime juice, jalapeno pepper
and salt. Add pasta, tomatoes,
yellow bell pepper, zucchini and
green onions; toss to coat well.
Garnish as desired. Cover;
refrigerate.

Makes 6 to 8 servings

Chili Mac 'n Cheddar

1 (7-ounce) package
  CREAMETTES® Elbow
  Macaroni
2 (15-ounce) cans chili with
  beans
1 (16-ounce) can whole
  tomatoes, undrained,
  chopped
1 (4-ounce) can diced green
  chilies or jalapeno
  peppers, drained
1 cup (4 ounces) shredded
  Cheddar cheese
Sour cream
Corn chips

Prepare CREAMETTES® Elbow
Macaroni according to package
directions; drain. In large skillet,
combine chili, tomatoes with
juice and green chilies; mix well.
Simmer 10 minutes. Stir in cooked
macaroni; sprinkle cheese over
top. Cover; simmer until cheese
melts, about 5 minutes. Serve with
sour cream and corn chips.
Refrigerate leftovers.

Makes 6 to 8 servings

Southwest Ruffle Salad

Turkey-Pasta Salad

4 cups cooked and drained wagon wheel or spiral pasta (about 2 cups uncooked)
2 cups short, thin, cooked turkey or chicken strips (about 8 ounces)
1 can (8 ounces) whole kernel corn, drained, *or* 1 cup frozen corn kernels, thawed
1 large zucchini, cut into ½-inch slices, each slice cut into quarters
1 large tomato, cut into ½-inch chunks
1 small red bell pepper, cut into ½-inch chunks
½ cup chopped cilantro or parsley
¾ cup PACE® Picante Sauce
⅓ cup reduced-calorie creamy garlic salad dressing
¼ teaspoon salt, optional
Additional PACE® Picante Sauce, optional

Combine pasta, turkey, corn, zucchini, tomato, red bell pepper and cilantro in large bowl. Combine ¾ cup picante sauce, dressing and salt in small bowl; mix well. Pour over pasta mixture; toss gently to coat. Refrigerate. Serve with additional picante sauce, if desired.

*Makes 6 servings,
about 8 cups salad*

Turkey-Pasta Salad

Warm Pasta and Spinach Salad

1 package (10 ounces) fresh spinach, washed, stems removed and torn into bite-size pieces
½ pound mushrooms, sliced
7 ounces MUELLER'S® Pasta Swirls®, cooked, rinsed with cold water and drained
1 medium red onion, sliced
6 slices uncooked bacon, coarsely chopped
1 tablespoon cornstarch
1 tablespoon sugar
1 teaspoon salt
½ teaspoon pepper
1 cup HELLMANN'S® or BEST FOODS® Real Mayonnaise
1 cup water
⅓ cup cider vinegar

In large serving bowl, toss spinach, mushrooms, pasta and red onion. In medium skillet, cook bacon over medium-high heat until crisp. Remove with slotted spoon. Pour off all but 2 tablespoons drippings. In small bowl, mix cornstarch, sugar, salt and pepper. With wire whisk, stir cornstarch mixture into drippings in skillet until smooth. Stir in mayonnaise until blended. Gradually stir in water and vinegar. Over medium heat, bring mixture to a boil; stir constantly. Boil 1 minute. Pour over spinach mixture. Add bacon; toss to coat well. Serve immediately.

Makes 8 to 10 servings

Italian Vegetable Soup

Italian Vegetable Soup

- 1 pound bulk Italian sausage
- 2 cups chopped onion
- 2 cloves garlic, finely chopped
- 7 cups water
- 4 medium carrots, pared and sliced
- 1 (28-ounce) can whole tomatoes, undrained, coarsely chopped
- 2 tablespoons WYLER'S® or STEERO® Beef-Flavor Instant Bouillon *or* 6 Beef-Flavor Bouillon Cubes
- 1 teaspoon Italian seasoning
- ¼ teaspoon pepper
- 1½ cups coarsely chopped zucchini
- 1 (15-ounce) can garbanzo beans, drained
- 1 cup uncooked CREAMETTE® Rotini or CREAMETTES® Elbow Macaroni

In large kettle or Dutch oven, brown sausage, onion and garlic; pour off fat. Add water, carrots, tomatoes with juice, bouillon, Italian seasoning and pepper; bring to a boil. Reduce heat; cover and simmer 30 minutes. Add zucchini, beans and rotini. Cook 15 to 20 minutes or until rotini is tender, stirring soup occasionally. Garnish as desired. Refrigerate leftovers.

Makes about 2½ quarts,
6 to 8 servings

Salmon Macaroni Salad

Salmon Macaroni Salad

1 (7-ounce) package *or* 2 cups uncooked CREAMETTE® Salad Macaroni Shells, cooked according to package directions and drained
2 hard-cooked eggs, chopped
1 (7¾-ounce) can salmon, drained, deboned and flaked
1 cup mayonnaise or salad dressing
¾ cup finely chopped celery
¼ cup chopped green bell pepper
1 (2-ounce) jar sliced pimiento, drained and chopped
2 tablespoons REALEMON® Lemon Juice from Concentrate
2 tablespoons sweet pickle relish
4 teaspoons WYLER'S® or STEERO® Chicken-Flavor Instant Bouillon
Lettuce

In large bowl, combine all ingredients except lettuce; mix well. Cover; chill. Stir before serving. Serve on lettuce; garnish as desired. Refrigerate leftovers.
Makes 4 to 6 servings

Turkey Meatball Soup

1 pound ground turkey
⅔ cup matzo meal
¼ cup EGG BEATERS® 99% Real Egg Product
2 tablespoons FLEISCHMANN'S® Sweet Unsalted Margarine
2 cloves garlic, minced
6 cups water
4 cups low-sodium tomato juice
1½ cups uncooked tri-color pasta twists
2 large carrots, peeled and thinly sliced
2 large tomatoes, chopped
1 large onion, chopped
1 tablespoon Italian seasoning
½ teaspoon ground black pepper
1 (10-ounce) package frozen chopped spinach, thawed

In small bowl, thoroughly mix turkey, matzo meal and egg product. Shape into 24 (1-inch) balls. In large saucepan over medium-high heat, brown meatballs, in batches, in margarine. Remove meatballs. In same saucepan, cook and stir garlic for 3 minutes or until browned. Add water, tomato juice, meatballs, pasta, carrots, tomatoes, onion, Italian seasoning and pepper. Heat to a boil. Cover; reduce heat. Simmer for 15 minutes. Add spinach; cook an additional 5 minutes or until pasta is tender.
Makes 10 (1½-cup) servings

Tangy Tortellini Salad

1 (8-ounce) can HUNT'S® Tomato Sauce
½ cup vegetable oil
⅓ cup red wine vinegar
½ teaspoon seasoned salt
¼ teaspoon *each* garlic powder, celery seed, black pepper and oregano
1 (7-ounce) box uncooked tortellini, cooked according to package directions, rinsed and drained
1 cup julienne-cut salami or ham
1 cup julienne-cut red bell peppers
1 (2-ounce) can pitted sliced ripe olives, drained
¼ cup chopped red onion
Lettuce leaves

In medium bowl, whisk together tomato sauce, oil, vinegar and seasonings. Cover; refrigerate until ready to use. In large bowl, combine tortellini, salami, red bell peppers, olives and onion. Arrange on lettuce leaves. Whisk dressing again; pour over pasta mixture.

Makes 4 to 6 servings

Tangy Tortellini Salad

Pasta, Chicken & Broccoli Pesto Toss

Cook pasta according to package directions until tender; drain and cool. Combine pasta, chicken, broccoli and mozzarella cheese in large bowl. Process basil and garlic in covered blender or food processor until finely chopped. Add mayonnaise, lemon juice and salt. Process to combine thoroughly. Stir in Parmesan cheese. Add to pasta mixture; toss to coat well. Stir in pine nuts. Serve immediately or cover and refrigerate. For maximum flavor, remove from refrigerator and toss gently 30 minutes before serving.

Makes 8 servings

Pasta, Chicken & Broccoli Pesto Toss

4 ounces (about 2 cups) uncooked vegetable spiral pasta
2 cups cubed, cooked chicken or turkey breast meat
2 cups small broccoli florets, cooked crisp-tender, cooled
1½ cups (6 ounces) SARGENTO® Preferred Light Fancy Supreme Shredded Mozzarella Cheese
⅔ cup lightly packed fresh basil leaves
2 cloves garlic
1 cup mayonnaise
1 tablespoon lemon juice
½ teaspoon salt
½ cup (1½ ounces) SARGENTO® Fancy Shredded Parmesan Cheese
½ cup pine nuts or coarsely chopped walnuts, toasted

Chicken Noodle Soup

1 (46-fluid ounce) can COLLEGE INN® Chicken Broth
½ pound boneless skinless chicken, cut into bite-size pieces
1½ cups uncooked medium egg noodles
1 cup sliced carrots
½ cup chopped onion
⅓ cup sliced celery
1 teaspoon dill weed
¼ teaspoon ground black pepper

In large saucepan, over medium-high heat, heat chicken broth, chicken, noodles, carrots, onion, celery, dill and pepper to a boil. Reduce heat; simmer 20 minutes or until chicken and noodles are cooked.

Makes 8 servings

Chicken Noodle Soup

Pasta and Walnut Fruit Salad

Pasta and Walnut Fruit Salad

½ (1-pound) package uncooked medium shell macaroni
1 (8-ounce) container plain nonfat yogurt
¼ cup frozen orange juice concentrate, thawed
1 (15-ounce) can juice-pack mandarin oranges, drained
1 cup seedless red grapes, halved
1 cup seedless green grapes, halved
1 apple, cored and chopped
½ cup sliced celery
½ cup walnut halves

Cook shells according to package directions; drain. In small bowl, blend yogurt and orange juice concentrate. In large bowl, combine shells and remaining ingredients. Add yogurt mixture; toss to coat. Cover; refrigerate.

Makes 6 to 8 servings

Favorite recipe from **Walnut Marketing Board**

Asian Noodle Salad

Prep time: 15 minutes
Cook time: 10 minutes

1 large DOLE® Fresh Pineapple
4 ounces uncooked vermicelli Sweet Soy Dressing (recipe follows)
1 can (8 ounces) water chestnuts, drained
2 cups bean sprouts
1 DOLE® Red Bell Pepper, seeded, slivered
1 cup chopped, unpeeled cucumber
½ cup chopped DOLE® Green Onion

• Twist crown from pineapple. Cut pineapple in half lengthwise with knife. Cut fruit from shells. Trim off core; cut fruit into chunks. Set aside 2 cups fruit; reserve remainder for another use.

• Cook vermicelli according to package directions; drain.

• Combine vermicelli and Sweet Soy Dressing in large bowl. Toss; let cool.

• Add 2 cups reserved pineapple and remaining ingredients. Toss to coat. *Makes 4 servings*

Sweet Soy Dressing

¼ cup white wine vinegar
3 tablespoons sugar
2 tablespoons vegetable oil
2 tablespoons sesame seeds, toasted
1 tablespoon soy sauce
1 teaspoon minced fresh ginger
1 clove garlic, pressed

Combine all ingredients in small bowl. Whisk to blend.

Marinated Shrimp & Pasta Salad

Lanai Pasta Salad

Prep time: 20 minutes

- 1 can (20 ounces) DOLE® Pineapple Chunks in Juice
- 3 cups cooked and drained spiral pasta
- 2 cups sugar peas or snow peas, trimmed
- 1 cup sliced DOLE® Carrots
- 1 cup sliced cucumber
- ¼ cup chopped cilantro or parsley
- ½ cup bottled reduced-calorie Italian salad dressing

• Drain pineapple; reserve ¼ cup juice.

• Combine pineapple, reserved juice and remaining ingredients in large bowl; toss to coat. Serve on salad greens, if desired.
Makes 6 to 8 servings

Lanai Pasta Salad

Marinated Shrimp & Pasta Salad

- 1 (7-ounce) package *or* 2 cups uncooked CREAMETTE® Salad Macaroni Shells, cooked according to package directions and drained
- 1 (4¼-ounce) can ORLEANS® Shrimp, drained and soaked as label directs
- ½ cup REALEMON® Lemon Juice from Concentrate
- ½ cup vegetable oil
- 1 (0.7-ounce) package Italian salad dressing mix
- 1 teaspoon prepared horseradish
- 1½ cups small broccoli flowerets
- 1½ cups sliced zucchini
- 1 cup coarsely shredded carrots
- ¼ cup chopped green onions
  Lettuce

In jar or cruet, combine REALEMON® Brand, oil, salad dressing mix and horseradish. In large bowl, combine pasta, shrimp, broccoli, zucchini, carrots and green onions; toss with dressing mixture. Cover; chill, stirring occasionally. Serve on lettuce. Refrigerate leftovers.
Makes 8 to 10 servings

Picnic Perfect Pasta Salad

Prep time: 20 minutes
Cook time: 10 minutes
Chill time: 2 hours

1 can (8 ounces) DOLE® Pineapple Chunks in Juice
2 tablespoons sesame oil
1 tablespoon honey
1 tablespoon soy sauce
1 tablespoon minced crystallized ginger
1 large clove garlic, pressed
2 cups cooked and drained spiral pasta
1 cup cooked chicken chunks*
2 tablespoons sliced DOLE® Green Onion
2 cups cooked DOLE® Broccoli florettes
⅓ cup DOLE® Red Bell Pepper strips
1 tablespoon sesame seeds, toasted

• Drain pineapple; reserve ⅓ cup juice for dressing.

• For dressing, in screw-top jar, combine ⅓ cup reserved juice, sesame oil, honey, soy sauce, ginger and garlic. Shake well.

• In large bowl, combine pineapple, pasta, chicken and onion. Toss with dressing to coat. Cover; refrigerate at least 2 hours.

• Just before serving, add broccoli and red bell pepper. Toss well. Sprinkle with sesame seeds.
Makes 4 servings

*Use deli chicken, if desired.

Easy Macaroni Salad

1 cup HELLMANN'S® or BEST FOODS® Real, Light or Cholesterol Free Reduced Calorie Mayonnaise
2 tablespoons vinegar
1 tablespoon prepared yellow mustard
1 teaspoon sugar
1 teaspoon salt
¼ teaspoon freshly ground black pepper
8 ounces uncooked elbow macaroni, cooked, rinsed with cold water and drained
1 cup sliced celery
1 cup chopped green or red bell pepper
¼ cup chopped onion

In large bowl, combine mayonnaise, vinegar, mustard, sugar, salt and black pepper. Add macaroni, celery, green bell pepper and onion; toss to coat well. Cover; refrigerate. Garnish as desired.
Makes about 8 servings

Note: If desired, add milk to dressing mixture for a creamier salad.

Picnic Perfect Pasta Salad

Left to right: Aegean Pasta Salad, Tuna Nouveau

Aegean Pasta Salad

1 cup HELLMANN'S® or BEST
    FOODS® Real Mayonnaise
⅓ cup milk
¼ cup lemon juice
¾ cup finely chopped fresh
    mint leaves
½ cup finely chopped fresh
    parsley
½ cup (2 ounces) crumbled
    feta cheese
1 teaspoon salt
½ teaspoon pepper
7 ounces MUELLER'S® Pasta
    Curls™, cooked, rinsed with
    cold water and drained
2 medium tomatoes, seeded
    and chopped
1 medium cucumber, seeded
    and chopped
1 cup sliced pitted ripe olives
3 green onions, sliced

In large bowl, stir mayonnaise,
milk, lemon juice, mint, parsley,
feta cheese, salt and pepper
until well mixed. Add pasta,
tomatoes, cucumber, olives and
green onions; toss to coat well.
Cover; refrigerate.

Makes 8 to 12 servings

Tuna Nouveau

1½ cups HELLMANN'S® or BEST
    FOODS® Real Mayonnaise
1 can (6½ ounces) tuna,
    drained
6 anchovies
3 tablespoons drained capers,
    divided
2 tablespoons lemon juice
8 ounces MUELLER'S® Elbow
    Macaroni, cooked, rinsed
    with cold water and
    drained
2 cups broccoli florets, cooked
    tender-crisp
1 cup sliced carrots, cooked
    tender-crisp

In covered blender or food
processor container, combine
mayonnaise, tuna, anchovies, 1
tablespoon capers and lemon
juice; blend until smooth. Stir in
remaining 2 tablespoons capers.
In large bowl, combine macaroni,
broccoli and carrots. Add
dressing mixture; toss to coat well.
Cover; refrigerate.

Makes 6 to 8 servings

Pasta Primavera Salad

Catalonian Stew

2 **boneless skinless chicken
breasts, cut into bite-size
pieces**
3 **ounces pepperoni, diced**
1 **tablespoon vegetable oil**
2 **cans (15 ounces each)
tomato sauce**
3 **cups chicken broth**
1 **cup pimiento-stuffed olives,
halved**
2 **tablespoons sugar**
8 **ounces uncooked rotini or
other shaped pasta**
⅓ **cup chopped parsley**
⅛ **teaspoon crushed saffron,
optional**
1 **cup (4 ounces) SARGENTO®
Shredded Mild or Sharp
Cheddar Cheese**
1 **cup (4 ounces) SARGENTO®
Shredded Monterey Jack
Cheese**

In Dutch oven, cook chicken and
pepperoni in oil over medium
heat until chicken is lightly
browned, about 5 minutes; drain.
Add tomato sauce, chicken
broth, olives and sugar. Bring to a
boil; reduce heat and simmer,
covered, 15 minutes. Return to a
boil. Add rotini, parsley and
saffron if desired; cover and cook
an additional 15 minutes or until
pasta is tender. Combine
Cheddar and Monterey Jack
cheeses in small bowl. Spoon
stew into 6 individual ovenproof
serving bowls; sprinkle evenly with
cheese. Bake in preheated 350°F
oven about 5 minutes until
cheese is melted.

Makes 6 servings

Pasta Primavera Salad

¾ **pound uncooked corkscrew
pasta, hot cooked and
drained**
3 **tablespoons olive or
vegetable oil**
2 **medium zucchini, cut into
¼-inch slices**
1 **cup broccoli flowerets,
steamed crisp-tender**
1 **large red or green bell
pepper, cut into small
chunks**
½ **cup cherry tomato halves**
⅓ **cup sliced radishes**
3 **green onions, chopped**
2 **tablespoons drained capers,
optional**
1 **cup prepared HIDDEN VALLEY
RANCH® Original Ranch®
Salad Dressing**

In large bowl, toss pasta with oil;
cool. Add remaining ingredients;
toss again. Cover; refrigerate at
least 2 hours. Just before serving;
add additional salad dressing, if
desired. *Makes 4 servings*

18

Bella Pasta Salad

- 6 ounces MUELLER'S® Rosettes™, cooked, rinsed with cold water and drained
- 8 ounces mozzarella cheese or smoked mozzarella, cut into 2-inch strips
- 1 cup cherry tomatoes, quartered
- 1 yellow bell pepper, cut into 2-inch strips
- 1 zucchini, cut into 2-inch strips
- ½ cup MAZOLA® Corn Oil
- 3 tablespoons white wine vinegar
- 2 tablespoons chopped fresh basil
- 1 clove garlic, minced or pressed
- 1 teaspoon salt
- ½ teaspoon black pepper

In large bowl, toss rosettes, cheese, tomatoes, yellow bell pepper and zucchini. In small bowl, stir corn oil, vinegar, basil, garlic, salt and black pepper until well mixed. Pour over pasta and vegetables; toss to coat well. Cover; refrigerate several hours.

Makes 12 servings

Bella Pasta Salad

Pasta Cheddar Cheese Salad

- 1 container (15 ounces) SARGENTO® Ricotta Cheese*
- 1 large cucumber, peeled, seeded and cut into bite-size pieces
- 1 green onion, thinly sliced
- 6 to 8 sprigs fresh parsley, stems removed
- 1 clove garlic
- ½ teaspoon salt
- ½ teaspoon white pepper
- 4 cups (16 ounces) uncooked pasta spirals or twists
- 2 small green or red bell peppers, cored, seeded and cut into ½-inch pieces
- 1 cup (4 ounces) SARGENTO® Shredded Cheddar Cheese
- Additional salt and white pepper to taste

Fit food processor with steel cutting blade. Add ricotta cheese, cucumber, green onion, parlsey, garlic, ½ teaspoon salt and ½ teaspoon white pepper. Process until well combined. Pour into large bowl.

Cook pasta according to package directions; drain. Immediately add hot pasta to bowl with dressing mixture. Stir to thoroughly coat pasta. Add bell peppers, Cheddar cheese and additional salt and white pepper; stir to coat. Serve immediately or cover and refrigerate up to 3 days. For maximum flavor, bring to room temperature before serving.   *Makes 8 servings*

*SARGENTO® Part-Skim Ricotta or Lite Ricotta can also be used.

Quick Beef Soup

- 1½ pounds lean ground beef
- 1 cup chopped onion
- 2 cloves garlic, finely chopped
- 1 can (28 ounces) tomatoes, undrained
- 6 cups water
- 6 beef bouillon cubes
- ¼ teaspoon pepper
- ½ cup uncooked orzo
- 1½ cups frozen peas, carrots and corn vegetable blend
- French bread, optional

Cook beef, onion and garlic in large saucepan over medium-high heat until beef is brown, stirring to separate meat; drain fat.

Process tomatoes with juice in covered blender or food processor until smooth. Add tomatoes, water, bouillon cubes and pepper to meat mixture. Bring to a boil; reduce heat to low. Simmer, uncovered, 20 minutes. Add orzo and vegetables. Simmer an additional 15 minutes. Serve with French bread if desired.

Makes 6 servings

Favorite recipe from **North Dakota Beef Commission**

Quick Beef Soup

Five-Way Cincinnati Chili

Prep time: 15 minutes
Cook time: 1 hour

1½ **pounds ground beef**
  1 **medium onion, finely chopped**
  2 **cloves garlic, minced**
  1 **can (28 ounces) Italian plum tomatoes, undrained**
  1 **cup water**
  2 **tablespoons chili powder**
  1 **tablespoon unsweetened cocoa powder**
  1 **teaspoon** *each* **salt, dry mustard, ground cumin and paprika**
  ¼ **teaspoon** *each* **ground red and black pepper**
  ⅛ **teaspoon** *each* **ground allspice, cardamom, cinnamon and cloves**
  8 **ounces uncooked vermicelli or thin spaghetti, hot cooked and drained**
  1 **can (15¼ ounces) red kidney beans, heated**
  1 **small onion, finely chopped**
  1 **cup (4 ounces) finely shredded Cheddar cheese**

Cook ground beef, chopped medium onion and garlic in Dutch oven over medium-high heat until beef is brown, stirring to separate meat. Drain fat. Stir in tomatoes with juice, water, chili powder, cocoa, salt, dry mustard, cumin, paprika, red and black pepper, allspice, cardamom, cinnamon and cloves. Bring to a boil; reduce heat and simmer, uncovered, 45 minutes. To serve chili, layer vermicelli, beans, chili mixture, chopped small onion and cheese on six individual plates.   *Makes 6 servings*

Note: To serve Four-Way Cincinnati Chili, layer vermicelli, chili mixture, chopped small onion and cheese on 6 individual plates; to serve Three-Way Cincinnati Chili, layer vermicelli, chili mixture and cheese on 6 individual plates.

Favorite recipe from **National Live Stock and Meat Board**

Five-Way Cincinnati Chili

Cheesy Cioppino

  ½ **pound sweet (mild) Italian sausage, thinly sliced**
  2 **tablespoons olive oil**
  1 **large onion, chopped**
  1 **medium green bell pepper, coarsely chopped**
  1 **large clove garlic, minced**
  2 **(16-ounce) cans beef broth**
  1 **can (28 ounces) tomatoes, undrained, chopped**
  1 **can (8 ounces) tomato sauce**
  ½ **cup dry red wine**
  1 **pound medium shrimp, shelled and deveined**
1½ **cups sliced zucchini**
  1 **cup sliced carrots**
  ¾ **cup diagonally sliced celery**
  2 **lobster tails, cooked, shelled and sliced into ½-inch pieces**
1½ **cups cooked and drained fusilli pasta**
  ¼ **cup chopped parsley**
  ½ **teaspoon dried basil, crushed**
  3 **cups (12 ounces) shredded Jarlsberg cheese**

Italian Pasta Salad

In large saucepan, brown sausage in oil. Add onion, green bell pepper and garlic. Cook and stir until onion is transparent. Add beef broth, tomatoes with juice, tomato sauce, wine, shrimp, zucchini, carrots and celery. Simmer until vegetables are tender and shrimp is cooked, about 10 minutes. Add lobster, pasta, parsley and basil; heat through.

To serve, spoon soup into 8 individual ovenproof crocks. Evenly top each with cheese. Broil, 4 to 5 inches from heat source, until cheese is melted and lightly browned.

Makes 8 servings

Favorite recipe from **Norseland Foods, Inc.**

Italian Pasta Salad

Prep time: 15 minutes

3 cups (8 ounces) uncooked tri-color rotini, cooked and drained
1 cup (4 ounces) KRAFT® 100% Grated Parmesan Cheese
1 (8-ounce) bottle KRAFT® House Italian Dressing
½ cup *each* chopped red bell pepper and red onion slices
2 cups broccoli flowerets
½ cup pitted ripe olive slices

• Mix together ingredients in large bowl until well blended. Chill.

Makes 8 cups

Tortellini Soup

Tortellini Soup

2 cloves garlic, crushed
1 tablespoon margarine
2 (13¾-fluid ounce) cans
 COLLEGE INN® Chicken or
 Beef Broth
1 (8-ounce) package fresh or
 frozen cheese tortellini,
 thawed
1 (10-ounce) package fresh or
 frozen spinach, thawed
1 (16-ounce) can stewed
 tomatoes, undrained,
 coarsely chopped
 Grated Parmesan cheese

In large saucepan over medium-high heat, cook and stir garlic in margarine for 2 to 3 minutes. Add broth and tortellini; heat to a boil. Reduce heat; simmer 10 minutes. Add spinach and tomatoes; simmer an additional 5 minutes. Serve topped with cheese.

Makes 6 servings

Linguine Summer Salad

3 tablespoons white wine
 vinegar
1 tablespoon Dijon-style
 mustard
1 tablespoon minced parsley
1 teaspoon dried basil leaves,
 crushed
 Freshly ground black pepper,
 to taste
½ cup olive oil
8 ounces uncooked linguine,
 cooked, drained and
 cooled
¼ pound prosciutto, ham or
 salami, cut into julienne
 strips
1 cup chopped cucumber,
 peeled and seeded, if
 desired
¾ cup sliced radishes
½ cup sliced pitted black
 olives
1 green onion, thinly sliced
1½ cups (6 ounces) SARGENTO®
 Preferred Light Fancy
 Supreme Shredded
 Mozzarella Cheese
½ cup (1½ ounces) SARGENTO®
 Fancy Shredded Parmesan
 Cheese

Combine vinegar, mustard, parsley, basil and pepper in large bowl. Gradually add oil, whisking until smooth and thickened. Add linguine, prosciutto, cucumber, radishes, olives, and onion; toss to combine. Add cheeses; toss again. Serve immediately or cover and refrigerate. For maximum flavor, remove from refrigerator and toss gently 30 minutes before serving.

Makes 8 servings

Note: If desired, about ¾ cup prepared Italian-style salad dressing may be substituted for dressing above.

Italian Chicken Salad

¾ cup plus 1 tablespoon vegetable oil
½ cup REALEMON® Lemon Juice from Concentrate
2 tablespoons grated Parmesan cheese
3 teaspoons WYLER'S® or STEERO® Chicken-Flavor Instant Bouillon
1 teaspoon sugar
½ teaspoon oregano leaves
1 clove garlic, finely chopped
⅛ teaspoon black pepper
1 pound boneless skinless chicken breasts, cut into strips
1 (9-ounce) package frozen artichoke hearts, cooked and drained
¼ (1-pound) package CREAMETTE® Linguine, cooked according to package directions and drained
1 cup sliced fresh mushrooms
½ cup chopped red bell pepper
¼ cup sliced pitted ripe olives
Lettuce

For dressing, in 1-pint jar with tight-fitting lid, combine ¾ cup vegetable oil, REALEMON® Brand, cheese, 2 teaspoons bouillon, sugar, oregano, garlic and black pepper; shake well. In large skillet, cook and stir chicken strips in remaining 1 tablespoon oil and 1 teaspoon bouillon until browned and tender. In large bowl, combine chicken, dressing mixture and remaining ingredients except lettuce; mix well. Cover; chill. Serve on lettuce. Garnish as desired. Refrigerate leftovers. **Makes 4 servings**

Italian Chicken Salad

SPEEDY SOUPS & SALADS

Chicken Salad Deluxe

1¼ cups prepared buttermilk
   salad dressing
½ cup mayonnaise
3 tablespoons half-and-half
1¾ teaspoons Beau Monde
   seasoning
1 teaspoon salt
½ teaspoon pepper
2 pounds chicken breasts,
   boned, skinned, cooked
   and cubed
10 ounces uncooked 100%
   semolina medium shell
   macaroni, cooked, rinsed,
   drained and cooled
3 cups diced celery
2½ cups seedless green grapes,
   cut lengthwise into halves
1 package (12 ounces)
   slivered almonds, reserve
   1 tablespoon for garnish
2 cans (2.25 ounces each)
   sliced water chestnuts,
   drained
½ cup chopped onion
   Lettuce leaves
   Parsley, optional
   Sliced star fruit, optional
   Cantaloupe slices

For dressing, combine salad
dressing, mayonnaise, half-and-
half, seasoning, salt and pepper
in small bowl; blend well. Cover;
refrigerate overnight to blend
flavors.

Combine chicken, shells, celery,
grapes, almonds, water chestnuts
and onion in large bowl. Pour
dressing mixture over salad; toss
gently to coat. Serve on lettuce.
Garnish with reserved almonds,
parsley and star fruit. Serve with
cantaloupe slices.

Makes 20 servings

Favorite recipe from **North Dakota
Wheat Commission**

Pasta Del Sol

Prep time: 15 minutes
Chill time: 1 hour

1 can (20 ounces) DOLE®
   Pineapple Chunks in Juice
1 can (11 ounces) DOLE®
   Mandarin Orange
   Segments, drained
8 ounces uncooked medium
   shell macaroni, cooked
   and drained
1½ cups slivered ham or
   Cheddar cheese
1 cup sliced DOLE® Carrots
1 cup frozen peas, thawed
1 small DOLE® Red Bell Pepper,
   chunked
   Zest and juice from 1 DOLE®
   Orange
½ cup vegetable oil
1 tablespoon sugar
1 tablespoon dried basil
   leaves, crumbled
¼ teaspoon black pepper
   Dash nutmeg

• Drain pineapple; reserve ½ cup
juice for dressing.

• Combine pineapple, orange
segments, pasta, ham, carrots,
peas and red bell pepper in large
bowl.

• For dressing, in small bowl,
combine reserved ½ cup
pineapple juice, orange zest and
orange juice; add remaining
ingredients. Pour over salad; toss
well to coat. Cover; refrigerate at
least one hour or overnight.

Makes 8 servings

Chicken Salad Deluxe

26

Beef & Pasta Salad

3 cups CREAMETTE® Rotini,
  cooked according to
  package directions and
  drained
1 pound boneless stir-fry beef
  strips
2 teaspoons WYLER'S® or
  STEERO® Beef-Flavor Instant
  Bouillon
2 tablespoons vegetable or
  olive oil
1 cup bottled Italian salad
  dressing
6 ounces Provolone cheese,
  cut into cubes
1 large green bell pepper, cut
  into strips
1 cup cherry tomato halves
½ cup sliced pitted ripe olives
  Grated Parmesan cheese,
  optional

Beef & Pasta Salad

In large skillet, brown beef and
1 teaspoon bouillon in oil; remove
from skillet. In large bowl,
combine beef, rotini, salad
dressing and remaining
1 teaspoon bouillon; let stand 15
minutes. Add Provolone, green
bell pepper, tomatoes and olives;
mix well. Cover; chill. Serve with
Parmesan cheese if desired.
Refrigerate leftovers.
Makes 4 servings

Dijon Asparagus Chicken Salad

1 cup HELLMANN'S® or BEST
  FOODS® Real Mayonnaise
2 tablespoons Dijon-style
  mustard
2 tablespoons lemon juice
1 teaspoon salt
½ teaspoon black pepper
6 ounces MEULLER'S® Twist Trio®,
  cooked, rinsed with cold
  water and drained
1 pound boneless skinless
  chicken breasts, cooked
  and cubed
1 package (10 ounces) frozen
  asparagus spears, thawed
  and cut into 2-inch pieces
1 red bell pepper, cut into
  1-inch squares

In large bowl, stir mayonnaise,
mustard, lemon juice, salt and
black pepper. Add pasta,
chicken, asparagus and red bell
pepper; toss to coat well. Cover;
refrigerate.   *Makes 6 servings*

Antipasto Salad

Antipasto Salad

1 cup MIRACLE WHIP® Salad
   Dressing
½ cup milk
2 (0.6-ounce) packages
   GOOD SEASONS® Zesty
   Italian Salad Dressing
   Mix
5⅓ cups (16 ounces) uncooked
   mostaccioli, cooked and
   drained
1 (8-ounce) package cotto
   salami slices, cut into
   strips
1 (8-ounce) package CASINO®
   Natural Low-Moisture Part-
   Skim Mozzarella Cheese,
   cubed
¾ cup *each* thin red bell
   pepper strips and thin
   zucchini strips
½ cup pitted ripe olives,
   drained, halved

• Mix together salad dressing,
milk, dressing mix and pasta in
large shallow bowl.

• Arrange remaining ingredients
over pasta mixture; cover and
chill.   *Makes 18 servings,*
                  about 14 cups

Turkey 'n Spaghetti Summer Salad

Turkey 'n Spaghetti Summer Salad

**10 ounces uncooked spaghetti
 1 medium zucchini, thinly
    sliced
 2 cups cut-up cooked turkey
 1 can (8 ounces) cut green
    beans, drained
18 cherry tomatoes, halved
⅓ cup sliced pitted ripe olives
 2 medium green onions,
    chopped
¼ cup grated Parmesan
    cheese
 1 teaspoon salt
⅔ cup olive oil
¼ cup white wine vinegar
 2 tablespoons water
 1 (0.6-ounce) packet Italian
    salad dressing mix**

Cook spaghetti according to package directions; drain and rinse with cold water. Meanwhile, in small saucepan, cook zucchini in small amount of boiling water just until tender. Rinse in cold water; drain. In large bowl, combine spaghetti, zucchini, turkey, green beans, tomatoes, olives and green onions. Sprinkle with Parmesan cheese and salt. In small jar or cruet combine oil, vinegar, water and salad dressing mix. Pour over spaghetti mixture; toss lightly to coat. Refrigerate several hours or overnight to blend flavors.

Makes 6 to 8 servings

Favorite recipe from **California Poultry Industry Federation**

Creamy Shell Soup

4 cups water
3 to 4 chicken pieces
1 cup diced onions
¼ cup chopped celery
¼ cup minced parsley *or*
    1 tablespoon dried parsley
    flakes
1 bay leaf
1 teaspoon salt
¼ teaspoon white pepper
2 medium potatoes, diced
4 to 5 green onions, chopped
3 chicken bouillon cubes
½ teaspoon seasoned salt
½ teaspoon poultry seasoning
4 cups milk
2 cups uncooked medium
    shell macaroni, cooked
    and drained
¼ cup butter or margarine
¼ cup all-purpose flour
    Ground nutmeg
    Chopped fresh parsley

Simmer water, chicken, diced onions, celery, minced parsley, bay leaf, salt and pepper in Dutch oven until chicken is tender. Remove bay leaf; discard. Remove chicken; cool. Remove skin and debone; coarsely chop chicken. Set aside.

Add potatoes, green onions, bouillon cubes, seasoned salt and poultry seasoning to broth. Simmer 15 minutes. Add milk, macaroni and chicken; return to simmer.

Melt butter over medium heat in small saucepan. Add flour, stirring constantly, until mixture begins to brown. Add to soup; blend well. Let soup stand 20 minutes to blend flavors. Season to taste. Garnish with nutmeg and chopped parsley.

Makes 8 servings

Favorite recipe from **North Dakota Wheat Commission**

Creamy Shell Soup

15-Minute Pasta Combo

Prep time: 5 minutes
Cook time: 10 minutes

**8 ounces uncooked spaghetti,
   broken in half**
**½ cup KRAFT® House Italian
   Dressing**
**2 large tomatoes, seeded and
   chopped**
**2 cups LOUIS RICH® Hickory
   Smoked Breast of Turkey
   cubes**
**1 cup (4 ounces) KRAFT®
   100% Grated Parmesan
   Cheese**

• Cook spaghetti according to package directions; drain.

• In same pan used to cook pasta, heat dressing over medium heat. Add pasta; toss until well coated.

• Add tomatoes, turkey and Parmesan cheese; toss lightly. Garnish as desired.

Makes 6 servings

Tuna Linguine

Prep time: 10 minutes
Cook time: 13 minutes

**1 (6½-ounce) can white
   albacore tuna, packed in
   water**
**6 tablespoons FILIPPO BERIO®
   Extra-Virgin Flavorful
   Olive Oil**
Juice of 1 lemon
½ cup chopped fresh parsley
¼ teaspoon black pepper
¼ teaspoon salt, optional
**¾ pound uncooked linguine
   (or any other pasta)**

1. Drain tuna. In small bowl, break tuna into chunks; add oil. Stir in lemon juice, parsley, pepper and salt until combined.

2. Cook pasta according to package directions; do not overcook. Drain.

3. Spoon tuna sauce over pasta in large bowl; toss gently to coat. Serve. ***Makes 4 servings***

Sweet Apricots and Roasted Chicken in Pasta

　1 (10-ounce) package
　　uncooked bow tie noodles
1½ cups half-and-half
　2 chicken breast halves,
　　boned, skinned, roasted
　　and sliced
　1 can (17 ounces) California
　　apricot halves, drained
　　and quartered
　⅓ cup chopped green onions
　2 tablespoons margarine
　　Salt and pepper

Cook noodles according to package directions; drain. In medium saucepan, simmer half-and-half for 4 minutes. Add chicken, apricots, onions and margarine; continue simmering for 2 minutes. Pour over pasta in large bowl; toss gently to coat. Season with salt and pepper to taste. Serve immediately.

Makes 4 servings

Favorite recipe from **California Apricot Advisory Board**

*Sweet Apricots and
Roasted Chicken in Pasta*

Spaghetti Twists with Spicy Fresh Salsa

　½ cup WISH-BONE® Italian or
　　Lite Italian Dressing,
　　divided
　1 pound boneless chicken
　　breasts, cut into thin strips
　4 teaspoons finely chopped
　　cilantro,* divided
　¼ teaspoon plus ⅛ teaspoon
　　ground cumin, divided
　1 medium onion, chopped
　8 small tomatoes, chopped**
　1 can (4 ounces) chopped
　　green chilies, undrained
　½ teaspoon sugar
　¼ teaspoon hot pepper sauce
12 ounces uncooked spaghetti
　　twists or fusilli pasta, hot
　　cooked and drained
　1 cup finely shredded
　　Monterey Jack or Cheddar
　　cheese (about 3 ounces)

In large skillet, heat 2 tablespoons Italian dressing. Cook and stir chicken, 1 teaspoon cilantro and ⅛ teaspoon cumin in dressing until chicken is cooked through and tender; set mixture aside. In same saucepan, heat 2 tablespoons Italian dressing; cook and stir onion in dressing 3 minutes or until onion is almost tender. Add tomatoes, green

*Substitute 2 teaspoons dried cilantro. Use ½ teaspoon with the chicken and 1½ teaspoons with the sauce.

**Substitute 1 can (28 ounces) crushed tomatoes.

chilies with liquid, sugar, hot pepper sauce, remaining ¼ cup Italian dressing and ¼ teaspoon cumin. Bring mixture to a boil; reduce heat and simmer about 20 minutes. Stir in cooked chicken mixture and remaining 3 teaspoons cilantro; heat through. To serve, spoon sauce over pasta and sprinkle with cheese.

Makes about 4 servings

Rotelle with Pork & Pepper Pasta Sauce

Spaghetti & Meatballs

    1 pound lean ground beef
    ¾ cup grated Parmesan cheese
    ½ cup finely chopped onion
    ½ cup fresh bread crumbs (1 slice)
    1 (26-ounce) jar CLASSICO® Pasta Sauce, any flavor
    1 egg
    2 teaspoons WYLER'S® or STEERO® Beef-Flavor Instant Bouillon
    1 teaspoon Italian seasoning
    8 ounces fresh mushrooms, sliced (about 2 cups)
    1 (1-pound) package CREAMETTE® Spaghetti, cooked according to package directions and drained

In large bowl, combine beef, cheese, onion, crumbs, *½ cup* pasta sauce, egg, bouillon and Italian seasoning; mix well. Shape into 1-inch balls. In large kettle or Dutch oven, brown meatballs; pour off fat. Stir in remaining pasta sauce and mushrooms; simmer uncovered 10 minutes or until hot. Serve over hot cooked spaghetti. Refrigerate leftovers.

Makes 6 to 8 servings

Rotelle with Pork & Pepper Pasta Sauce

    ½ *each* green and red bell pepper, cut into strips
    1 medium onion, cut into wedges
    3 tablespoons olive oil
    1 (¾- to 1-pound) pork tenderloin, cut into ½-inch cubes
    2 cloves garlic, finely chopped
    1 (26-ounce) jar CLASSICO® Di Roma Arrabbiata (Spicy Red Pepper) Pasta Sauce
    ¼ teaspoon thyme leaves
    ½ (1-pound) package CREAMETTE® Rotelle, cooked according to package directions and drained

In large skillet, cook and stir bell peppers and onion in *2 tablespoons* oil until tender-crisp; remove. In same skillet, over high heat, cook and stir pork and garlic until browned. Add pasta sauce and thyme; simmer uncovered 20 minutes or until pork is tender, stirring occasionally. Add vegetables. Toss hot cooked rotelle with remaining *1 tablespoon* oil. Serve with sauce. Refrigerate leftovers.

Makes 4 to 6 servings

Shrimp Fettuccine

Shrimp Fettuccine

1½ cups prepared HIDDEN
    VALLEY RANCH® Original
    Ranch Salad Dressing
¼ cup sour cream
¼ cup grated Parmesan
    cheese
½ pound uncooked fettuccine,
    hot cooked and drained
½ pound cooked shrimp,
    shelled and deveined
½ cup cooked peas
    Additional Parmesan cheese,
    optional

In small bowl, combine salad
dressing, sour cream and ¼ cup
Parmesan cheese. In large bowl,
toss fettuccine with dressing
mixture, shrimp and peas. Divide
equally among 4 plates. Sprinkle
with additional Parmesan
cheese, if desired.

Makes 4 to 6 servings

Chicken Spaghetti Supreme

2 cups cubed cooked chicken
½ cup chopped green bell
    pepper
½ cup chopped onion
¼ cup margarine or butter
¼ to ⅓ cup unsifted flour
3 cups BORDEN® or MEADOW
    GOLD® Milk
4 teaspoons WYLER'S® or
    STEERO® Chicken-Flavor
    Instant Bouillon *or*
    4 Chicken-Flavor Bouillon
    Cubes
1 (4-ounce) can sliced
    mushrooms, drained
2 tablespoons chopped
    pimiento
1 (1-pound) package
    CREAMETTE® Spaghetti,
    cooked according to
    package directions and
    drained
    Grated Parmesan cheese,
    optional

In medium saucepan, cook
green pepper and onion in
margarine until tender. Stir in flour
until blended; gradually add milk
and bouillon. Cook and stir until
bouillon dissolves and mixture
begins to boil. Stir in chicken,
mushrooms and pimiento; heat
through. Serve over hot spaghetti;
top with Parmesan cheese if
desired. Refrigerate leftovers.

Makes 6 to 8 servings

Sausage Fettuccine

- **8 ounces uncooked fettuccine**
- **¼ cup butter or margarine**
- **½ pound fresh mushrooms, sliced**
- **1 clove garlic, minced**
- **1 pound ECKRICH® Smoked Sausage, cut diagonally into ¼-inch slices**
- **2 eggs, beaten**
- **½ cup heavy cream or half-and-half**
- **1 cup grated Parmesan cheese**
- **½ cup chopped fresh parsley**

Cook fettuccine according to package directions; drain. Melt butter in large skillet over medium heat. Add mushrooms and garlic; cook and stir until mushrooms are soft. Remove from skillet; set aside. In same skillet, heat sausage over medium heat until lightly browned. Drain any excess drippings. Return mushroom mixture to skillet. In small bowl, combine eggs and cream. Add to skillet mixture; continue heating just until cream mixture is hot. *Do not boil.* Add fettuccine; toss to combine. Mix in cheese and parsley. Serve immediately.

Makes 6 to 7 servings

Sausage Fettuccine

Crabmeat with Herbs and Pasta

- **1 small onion, minced**
- **1 carrot, shredded**
- **1 clove garlic, minced**
- **⅓ cup olive oil**
- **3 tablespoons butter or margarine**
- **6 ounces canned crabmeat, drained and flaked**
- **¼ cup chopped fresh basil *or* 1 teaspoon dried basil leaves, crushed**
- **2 tablespoons chopped parsley**
- **1 tablespoon lemon juice**
- **½ cup chopped pine nuts, optional**
- **½ teaspoon salt**
- **½ package (8 ounces) uncooked vermicelli, hot cooked and drained**

Cook and stir onion, carrot and garlic in hot oil and butter in large skillet over medium-high heat until vegetables are tender, but not brown. Reduce heat to medium. Stir in crabmeat, basil, parsley and lemon juice. Cook 4 minutes, stirring constantly. Stir in pine nuts and salt. Pour sauce over vermicelli in large bowl; toss gently to coat. Garnish as desired.   ***Makes 4 servings***

Favorite recipe from **New Jersey Department of Agriculture**

Crabmeat with Herbs and Pasta

Vegetable 'n Chicken Alfredo

Vegetable 'n Chicken Alfredo

- **4 tablespoons butter or margarine, divided**
- **3 tablespoons flour**
- **3 cups milk**
- **¾ cup (3 ounces) SARGENTO® Grated Cheese***
- **½ teaspoon dried basil, crushed**
- **¼ teaspoon salt**
- **¼ teaspoon black pepper**
- **1 tablespoon vegetable oil**
- **3 chicken breast halves, boned, skinned and cut into thin strips**
- **¼ cup thinly sliced green onions**
- **4 cups sliced fresh vegetables (broccoli, mushrooms, green or red bell peppers, celery, green beans, carrots or zucchini)**
- **½ pound uncooked pasta, hot cooked and drained**

In medium saucepan, melt 2 tablespoons butter. Add flour; cook over low heat 2 minutes, stirring occasionally. Gradually whisk in milk. Bring to a simmer; cook over medium heat until thickened, stirring constantly. Stir in Grated Cheese, basil, salt and black pepper. Set aside; keep warm.

Heat remaining 2 tablespoons butter and oil in large frying pan. Add chicken; cook over medium heat, stirring constantly until cooked through. Remove chicken from pan; set aside.

In same pan, cook green onions and other vegetables until crisp-tender, about 5 minutes. Toss vegetables with hot pasta and chicken in large bowl. Serve with sauce and additional Grated Cheese if desired.

Makes 4 servings

*SARGENTO® Parmesan, Parmesan and Romano or Italian-Style Grated Cheese may also be used.

Scallops with Vermicelli

1 pound bay scallops
2 tablespoons fresh lemon
    juice
2 tablespoons chopped
    parsley
1 onion, chopped
1 clove garlic, minced
2 tablespoons olive oil
2 tablespoons butter, divided
1½ cups canned Italian
    tomatoes, undrained and
    cut up
2 tablespoons chopped fresh
    basil or ½ teaspoon dried
    basil, crushed
¼ teaspoon dried oregano
    leaves, crushed
¼ teaspoon dried thyme
    leaves, crushed
2 tablespoons heavy cream
    Dash ground nutmeg
12 ounces uncooked vermicelli,
    hot cooked and drained

Rinse scallops. Combine scallops, juice and parsley in glass dish. Cover; marinate in refrigerator while preparing sauce.

Cook and stir onion and garlic in oil and 1 tablespoon butter in large skillet over medium-high heat until onion is tender. Add tomatoes with juice, basil, oregano and thyme. Reduce heat to low. Cover; simmer 30 minutes, stirring occasionally.

Drain scallops; cook and stir in remaining 1 tablespoon butter in another large skillet over medium heat until scallops are opaque, about 2 minutes. Add cream, nutmeg and tomato sauce mixture.

Pour sauce over vermicelli in large bowl; toss gently to coat. Garnish as desired.

Makes 4 servings

Favorite recipe from **New Jersey Department of Agriculture**

Chicken & Spaghetti Di Napoli

6 slices bacon
6 boneless skinless chicken
    breast halves (about
    1½ pounds)
1 cup thinly sliced carrots
1 clove garlic, finely chopped
1 (26-ounce) jar CLASSICO®
    Di Napoli (Tomato & Basil)
    Pasta Sauce
1 (1-pound) package
    CREAMETTE® Spaghetti
2 tablespoons olive or
    vegetable oil

In large skillet, cook bacon until crisp. Reserve 2 tablespoons drippings; drain and crumble bacon. In same skillet, brown chicken in reserved 2 tablespoons drippings; remove. Add carrots and garlic; cook and stir until tender-crisp. Add pasta sauce and chicken. Simmer, uncovered, 10 to 15 minutes or until chicken is tender. Meanwhile, cook spaghetti according to package directions; drain. Toss with oil. Slice chicken; serve on hot cooked spaghetti tossed with sauce. Garnish with crumbled bacon. Refrigerate leftovers.

Makes 6 servings

Scallops with Vermicelli

Mostaccioli and Sausage

- **1½ pounds link Italian sausage, sliced**
- **1 cup chopped onion**
- **¾ cup chopped green bell pepper**
- **2 (26-ounce) jars CLASSICO® Pasta Sauce, any flavor**
- **½ cup grated Parmesan cheese**
- **1 (1-pound) package CREAMETTE® Mostaccioli, cooked according to package directions and drained**
- **2 tablespoons olive oil**

In large saucepan, brown sausage; pour off fat. Add onion and pepper; cook and stir until tender. Add pasta sauce and Parmesan cheese. Bring to a boil; reduce heat. Cover and simmer 15 minutes, stirring occasionally. Toss hot cooked mostaccioli with oil. Serve with sauce. Garnish as desired. Refrigerate leftovers.

Makes 6 to 8 servings

Mostaccioli and Sausage

Cajun Shrimp Fettuccine

Prep time: 10 minutes
Cook time: 20 minutes

- **4 to 6 ounces uncooked fettuccine**
- **½ pound medium shrimp, shelled and deveined**
- **2 slices bacon, diced**
- **2 cloves garlic, minced**
- **⅛ to ¼ teaspoon ground red pepper, or to taste**
- **1 can (14½ ounces) DEL MONTE® Cajun or Original Recipe Stewed Tomatoes,* undrained**
- **1 can (8 ounces) DEL MONTE® Tomato Sauce**
- **1 green bell pepper, cut into thin strips**

Cook pasta according to package directions; drain. Cut shrimp in half lengthwise. In large skillet, cook bacon until crisp; drain. Stir in garlic and ground red pepper; cook and stir 1 minute. Add stewed tomatoes with juice and tomato sauce. Cook, uncovered, over medium heat 10 minutes, stirring occasionally. Add shrimp and green bell pepper; cook 2 to 3 minutes or until shrimp are pink. Just before serving, spoon sauce over hot fettuccine.

Makes 4 servings

*If using Original Recipe Tomatoes, add a pinch each of ground cinnamon, ground cloves and ground red pepper to tomato mixture; continue as directed.

Hint: After deveining shrimp, rinse thoroughly under cold water; drain.

Ham Pasta Primavera

Ham Pasta Primavera

- 3 tablespoons unsalted margarine or butter, divided
- 1 cup pea pods
- ½ cup shredded carrots
- 1 small red pepper, cut into strips
- 3 green onions, sliced
- ¾ cup evaporated skim milk
- 3 cups (12 ounces) ARMOUR® Lower Salt Ham, cut into cubes
- 10 ounces uncooked spaghetti, hot cooked and drained
  Fresh basil, cilantro and freshly ground black pepper, optional

Melt 1 tablespoon margarine in medium saucepan over medium heat. Add vegetables; cook and stir until tender. Add remaining 2 tablespoons margarine, milk and ham. Cook over medium-high heat 3 to 4 minutes, or until mixture thickens slightly. Serve over warm spaghetti. Garnish with fresh basil, cilantro and freshly ground black pepper, if desired.

Makes 4 to 6 servings

San Antonio-Style Turkey-Pasta Skillet

pasta is tender and most of liquid is absorbed, 4 to 5 minutes. Sprinkle with cheese and cilantro. Serve with additional picante sauce and garnish, if desired.

Makes 6 servings

Fettuccine with Tomatoes and Zucchini

Prep time: 6 minutes
Cook time: 20 minutes

6 ounces uncooked fettuccine, hot cooked and drained
½ pound ground beef
½ onion, chopped
1 teaspoon dried tarragon, crushed
1 can (14½ ounces) DEL MONTE® Original Recipe Stewed Tomatoes, undrained
1 can (8 ounces) DEL MONTE® Tomato Sauce
1 medium carrot, cut into julienne strips
1 medium zucchini, cubed
Chopped parsley

In large skillet, brown beef with onion and tarragon; drain fat. Add stewed tomatoes with juice, tomato sauce and carrots. Cook, uncovered, over medium heat 8 minutes, stirring occasionally. Add zucchini; cover and cook 7 minutes or until zucchini is tender. Just before serving, spoon sauce over hot pasta. Garnish with chopped parsley, if desired.

Makes 4 to 6 servings

Hint: Pasta may be cooked ahead and rinsed in cold water. Freeze or refrigerate; reheat in boiling water or microwave oven.

San Antonio-Style Turkey-Pasta Skillet

2 large onions, coarsely chopped (2 cups)
2 cloves garlic, minced
¼ cup vegetable oil
10 ounces uncooked vermicelli, broken into pieces
2 cups diced cooked turkey or chicken
1 can (16 ounces) whole tomatoes, undrained
1 can (about 14 ounces) chicken broth
¾ cup PACE® Picante Sauce
1 teaspoon ground cumin
1 large green bell pepper, cut into short, thin strips
½ cup (2 ounces) shredded Cheddar cheese
¼ cup chopped cilantro, optional
Additional PACE® Picante Sauce, optional

Cook and stir onion and garlic in oil in 12-inch skillet over medium heat 2 minutes. Add pasta; cook and stir 2 minutes. Stir in turkey, tomatoes with juice, broth, ¾ cup picante sauce and cumin. Simmer, stirring occasionally and breaking up tomatoes with spoon, 3 minutes. Add green bell pepper; continue to simmer until

Green and Gold Fettuccine with Salmon

2 cans (6½ ounces each) salmon,* drained
2 tablespoons olive oil
2 cloves garlic, minced
¼ cup minced parsley
2 teaspoons minced fresh oregano or ½ teaspoon dried oregano, crumbled
2 teaspoons minced fresh basil or ½ teaspoon dried basil, crumbled
¼ teaspoon coarsely ground black pepper
4 ounces each uncooked plain and spinach fettuccine, hot cooked and drained
2 teaspoons lemon juice
Blanched matchstick carrots, asparagus spears or broccoli florets, optional
Grated Parmesan cheese

Place salmon in medium bowl. With fork, break into large chunks and debone; remove skin, if desired. Heat oil in large skillet over medium-high heat until hot. Cook and stir garlic in hot oil until golden. Add parsley, oregano, basil and pepper; cook and stir 30 seconds. Pour half of herb sauce over fettuccine; toss gently to coat. Arrange on large, heated platter; keep warm.

Add salmon and lemon juice to remaining sauce. Heat, stirring gently, just until salmon is hot. Spoon over hot fettuccine. Garnish with vegetables, if desired. Serve with Parmesan cheese. *Makes 6 servings*

*Canned tuna may be substituted for the salmon.

Favorite recipe from **National Fisheries Institute**

Clams with Red Peppers and Pasta

3 dozen littleneck or cherrystone clams, scrubbed
Water
¼ cup vinegar
1 clove garlic, minced
1 hot red chili pepper, minced or ⅛ teaspoon ground red pepper
2 tablespoons olive oil
2 tablespoons butter or margarine
2 large red bell peppers, diced
½ teaspoon salt
½ teaspoon chopped fresh rosemary
½ teaspoon fresh thyme leaves
¼ teaspoon black pepper
8 ounces uncooked spinach linguine or other pasta, hot cooked and drained

Place clams in large bowl. Cover with water; add vinegar. Let stand 30 minutes; drain and rinse. Cook and stir garlic and hot red pepper in oil and butter in large skillet over medium-high heat 1 minute. Stir in clams, red bell peppers, salt, rosemary, thyme and black pepper. Reduce heat to low. Simmer, covered, 4 minutes or until clams open. (Discard any clams that do not open.) Serve over linguine. Garnish as desired.
Makes 4 servings

Favorite recipe from **Virginia Marine Products Board**

An Early Spring Pasta

1 cup Oriental Dressing (recipe follows)
8 ounces cooked turkey breast, cut into julienne strips
4 ounces carrots, cut into julienne strips
4 ounces asparagus, diagonally sliced into 1-inch pieces
4 ounces fresh spinach, chopped
12 ounces uncooked linguine, hot cooked and drained

Heat Oriental Dressing in large saucepan over high heat to a boil. Add turkey, carrots, asparagus and spinach; reduce heat to medium. Cook 2 to 3 minutes. Pour sauce over linguine in large bowl; toss gently to coat.

Makes 4 to 6 servings

Oriental Dressing

1 large onion, sliced
1 cup water
¼ cup *each* soy sauce and rice vinegar
1 tablespoon *each* garlic and ginger root, minced
1 tablespoon *each* sesame oil and lemon juice
1½ teaspoons *each* sugar and pepper
1½ teaspoons hot pepper sauce
2 tablespoons cornstarch
¼ cup water

Spread onion on large baking pan. Heat in preheated 400°F oven until edges are dark brown, about 15 minutes. Process onion in covered food processor until smooth. Place onion and remaining ingredients except cornstarch and ¼ cup water in medium saucepan. Bring to a boil. Combine cornstarch and ¼ cup water in cup until smooth. Gradually stir into dressing mixture. Heat until mixture boils, stirring constantly. Reduce heat to low; simmer 2 to 3 minutes.

Favorite recipe from **National Pasta Association**

Creamy Chicken Fettuccine

1 jar (12 ounces) HEINZ® HomeStyle Chicken Gravy
1 package (4 ounces) garlic and spice *or* herb and garlic flavored soft spreadable cheese
2 cups cubed cooked chicken
2 cups hot cooked and drained spinach fettuccine (about 8 ounces uncooked)
Snipped fresh chives, basil, thyme or tarragon

Combine gravy and cheese in 2-quart saucepan. Cook and stir over medium heat until cheese melts and sauce is smooth. Stir in chicken; cook until heated through. Serve over fettuccine. Sprinkle with chives.

Makes 4 servings

Meatballs and Pasta Picante con Queso

1 pound ground beef
1 cup fresh bread crumbs (about 2 slices bread)
¾ cup PACE® Picante Sauce, divided
¼ cup minced onion
2 tablespoons minced parsley
1 egg
1 teaspoon salt
2 teaspoons ground cumin, divided
1 can (15 ounces) tomato sauce
½ pound pasteurized process cheese spread, cubed
1½ teaspoons chili powder
1 teaspoon ground coriander
1 pound uncooked thin linguine or other pasta, hot cooked and drained
⅓ cup chopped fresh cilantro, optional
Additional PACE® Picante Sauce, optional

Combine beef, bread crumbs, ¼ cup picante sauce, onion, parsley, egg, salt and ½ teaspoon cumin; mix well. Shape into 1-inch balls. Place meatballs on 15 × 10-inch jelly roll pan. Bake at 350°F for 15 minutes. Drain off fat. (Or, arrange meatballs in a circle in 9-inch glass pie plate. Cover with waxed paper; microwave at HIGH (100% power) 3 minutes, rotating dish halfway through cooking. Drain off fat; repeat until all meatballs are cooked.)

Combine tomato sauce, remaining ½ cup picante sauce, cheese spread, chili powder, remaining 1½ teaspoons cumin and coriander in large saucepan. Cook over low heat, stirring frequently until cheese is melted. Add meatballs; simmer until heated through. Spoon over pasta; sprinkle with cilantro, if desired. Serve with additional picante sauce and garnish, if desired. **Makes 6 servings**

Meatballs and Pasta Picante con Queso

Garlic Shrimp with Noodles

4 tablespoons butter, divided
¼ cup finely chopped onion
2 cups water
1 package LIPTON® Noodles &
    Sauce — Butter & Herb
2 tablespoons olive oil
1 tablespoon finely chopped
    garlic
1 pound raw medium shrimp,
    cleaned
1 can (14 ounces) artichoke
    hearts, drained and
    halved
¼ cup finely chopped parsley
    Pepper to taste
    Watercress, optional

In medium saucepan, melt 2 tablespoons butter; add onion and cook until tender. Add water; bring to a boil. Stir in noodles and butter & herb sauce; continue boiling over medium heat, stirring occasionally, 8 minutes or until noodles are tender.

Meanwhile, in large skillet, heat remaining 2 tablespoons butter with olive oil; cook garlic over medium-high heat 30 seconds. Add shrimp and artichokes; cook, stirring occasionally, 3 minutes or until shrimp turn pink. Stir in parsley and pepper. To serve, combine shrimp mixture with hot noodles. Garnish, if desired, with watercress.

Makes about 4 servings

To Microwave: In 2-quart microwave-safe casserole, microwave 2 tablespoons butter with onion, uncovered, at HIGH (100% Power) 2 minutes or until tender. Stir in water, noodles and butter & herb sauce; microwave 11 minutes or until noodles are tender. Stir; cover and set aside.

Garlic Shrimp with Noodles

In 1-quart microwave-safe casserole or 9-inch glass pie plate, microwave remaining 2 tablespoons butter, olive oil and garlic at HIGH 2 minutes. Stir in shrimp and artichokes; microwave 3 minutes or until shrimp are almost pink, stirring once. Stir in parsley and pepper. Combine shrimp mixture with noodles and microwave, covered, 1 minute at HIGH or until heated through. Let stand, covered, 2 minutes.

Chunky Pasta Sauce with Meat

6 ounces ground beef
6 ounces mild or hot Italian sausage, sliced
½ medium onion, coarsely chopped
1 clove garlic, minced
2 cans (14½ ounces each) DEL MONTE® Chunky Pasta Recipe Stewed Tomatoes, undrained
1 can (8 ounces) DEL MONTE® Tomato Sauce
¼ cup red wine, optional
Hot cooked pasta
Grated Parmesan cheese

In large saucepan, brown beef and sausage; drain all but 1 tablespoon drippings. Add onion and garlic; cook until tender. Add stewed tomatoes with juice, tomato sauce and wine. Boil, uncovered, 15 minutes, stirring frequently. Serve over pasta; top with Parmesan cheese.

Makes 4 servings
(4 cups sauce)

Variation: Serve sauce over vegetables, omelets or frittatas.

Chunky Pasta Sauce with Meat

Pasta with Chicken and Peppers

Prep time: 15 minutes
Cook time: 25 minutes

5 tablespoons FILIPPO BERIO® Extra-Virgin Flavorful Olive Oil, divided
1 large boneless chicken breast, skinned and cut into julienne strips (1 pound)
1 medium onion, chopped
1 medium red bell pepper, cut into julienne strips
1 medium green bell pepper, cut into julienne strips
1 clove garlic, minced
⅛ teaspoon ground red pepper
2 large tomatoes, chopped
¾ pound uncooked pasta tubes, such as penne

1. Heat 2 tablespoons olive oil over medium heat in large skillet. Cook and stir chicken until tender. Remove chicken; set aside.

2. Add 2 tablespoons olive oil to skillet; cook and stir onion and bell peppers until tender.

3. Return chicken to pan; add garlic and ground red pepper. Cook for 3 minutes, stirring constantly.

4. Add tomatoes; simmer for 10 minutes.

5. While chicken mixture is simmering, cook pasta according to package directions; do not overcook. Drain and toss with remaining 1 tablespoon olive oil in large bowl. Serve with sauce.

Makes 4 servings

Tortellini with Three-Cheese Tuna Sauce

Tortellini with Three-Cheese Tuna Sauce

Prep time: 25 minutes

- 1 pound uncooked spinach or egg cheese-filled tortellini
- 2 green onions, thinly sliced
- 1 clove garlic, minced
- 1 tablespoon butter or margarine
- 1 cup lowfat ricotta cheese
- ½ cup lowfat milk
- 1 can (9¼ ounces) STARKIST® Tuna, drained and broken into chunks
- ½ cup (2 ounces) shredded lowfat mozzarella cheese
- ¼ cup grated Parmesan or Romano cheese
- 2 tablespoons chopped fresh basil *or* 2 teaspoons dried basil, crushed
- 1 teaspoon grated lemon peel
  Fresh tomato wedges, red peppers and basil leaves for garnish, optional

In large saucepan, cook tortellini in boiling salted water according to package directions. When tortellini is nearly done, in another large saucepan cook and stir onions and garlic in butter for 2 minutes. Whisk in ricotta cheese and milk. Add tuna, cheeses, basil and lemon peel. Cook over medium-low heat until mixture is heated and cheeses are melted.

Drain pasta; add to sauce. Toss well to coat; garnish if desired. Serve immediately.
Makes 4 to 5 servings

Lazy Lasagna

- 1 pound ground beef
- 1 jar (32 ounces) spaghetti sauce
- 1 pound cottage cheese
- 8 ounces sour cream
- 8 uncooked lasagna noodles
- 3 packages (6 ounces each) sliced mozzarella cheese (12 slices)
- ½ cup grated Parmesan cheese
- 1 cup water

Cook beef in large skillet over medium-high heat until meat is brown, stirring to separate meat; drain fat. Add spaghetti sauce. Reduce heat to low. Heat through, stirring occasionally; set aside. Combine cottage cheese and sour cream in medium bowl; blend well.

Spoon 1½ cups meat sauce in bottom of 13 × 9-inch pan. Place ½ the uncooked noodles over sauce, then ½ the cheese mixture, 4 slices mozzarella, ½ the remaining meat sauce and ¼ cup Parmesan cheese. Repeat layers starting with noodles. Top with remaining 4 slices mozzarella cheese. Pour water around sides of pan. Cover tightly with foil. Bake in preheated 350°F oven 1 hour. Uncover; bake 20 minutes more or until bubbly. Let stand 15 to 20 minutes. Garnish as desired.

Makes 8 to 10 servings

Favorite recipe from **North Dakota Dairy Promotion Commission**

Chicken Pesto

- 4 boneless skinless chicken breast halves (about 1 pound)
- 1½ tablespoons olive oil
- 1 jar (12 ounces) HEINZ® HomeStyle Chicken Gravy
- ¼ cup water
- 2 tablespoons prepared pesto sauce
- 2 teaspoons lemon juice
- 3 cups hot cooked pasta
- 2 tablespoons grated Parmesan cheese

In large skillet, cook chicken in oil until brown on both sides. Cover; cook 6 to 8 minutes or until chicken is tender. Remove chicken; keep warm. Combine gravy, water, pesto and lemon juice in same skillet; heat until bubbly, stirring occasionally. To serve, place chicken on pasta; spoon sauce over chicken and sprinkle with cheese.

Makes 4 servings

Lazy Lasagna

Classic Stuffed Shells

Classic Stuffed Shells

18 CREAMETTE® Jumbo
    Macaroni Shells, cooked
    according to package
    directions and drained
½ pound lean ground beef
⅔ cup chopped onion
1 clove garlic, chopped
1 (26-ounce) jar CLASSICO®
    Di Napoli (Tomato & Basil)
    Pasta Sauce
1½ teaspoons oregano leaves
1 teaspoon WYLER'S® or
    STEERO® Beef-Flavor Instant
    Bouillon
1 (16-ounce) container
    BORDEN® or MEADOW
    GOLD® Cottage Cheese
2 cups (8 ounces) shredded
    mozzarella cheese
½ cup grated Parmesan
    cheese
1 egg

In large skillet, brown beef, onion
and garlic; pour off fat. Stir in
pasta sauce, oregano and
bouillon; simmer 10 minutes. In
large bowl, mix cottage cheese,
1 cup mozzarella cheese,
Parmesan cheese and egg. Stuff
shells with cheese mixture. In
13 × 9-inch baking dish or
individual ramekins, pour about
half the sauce mixture; arrange
stuffed shells in sauce. Top with
remaining sauce; cover. Bake in
preheated 350° oven 30 minutes.
Uncover; sprinkle with remaining
1 cup mozzarella cheese. Bake 3
minutes longer. Refrigerate
leftovers.

Makes 6 to 8 servings

Veal Scallopine

1 tablespoon flour
½ teaspoon salt
    Dash pepper
4 veal cutlets (1 pound)
¼ cup CRISCO® Shortening
½ onion, thinly sliced
1 can (14½ ounces) tomatoes,
    undrained
1 can (4 ounces) sliced
    mushrooms, undrained
1 tablespoon chopped parsley
1 tablespoon capers, drained
¼ teaspoon garlic salt
¼ teaspoon dried oregano,
    crushed
    Hot buttered noodles

Combine flour, salt and pepper;
coat veal lightly with mixture. In
medium skillet, brown veal slowly
in hot CRISCO®. Remove veal
from skillet. Add onion; cook until
tender but not brown. Add veal,
tomatoes with juice, undrained
mushrooms, parsley, capers,
garlic salt and oregano. Cover;
simmer until veal is tender, 20 to
30 minutes, stirring occasionally.
Arrange veal over noodles; top
with sauce.   *Makes 4 servings*

Spinach-Cheese Lasagna Rolls

½ cup chopped onion
1 clove garlic, minced
1 tablespoon olive or
vegetable oil
1 can (15 ounces) whole leaf
spinach, well drained,
finely chopped
1 cup lowfat ricotta cheese
½ cup grated Parmesan
cheese
1 egg
1 teaspoon sugar
⅛ teaspoon pepper
6 lasagna noodles, cooked
and drained
2 cans (8 ounces each) no salt
added tomato sauce
1 can (4 ounces) no salt
added mushroom pieces
and stems, drained
1 teaspoon dried basil leaves,
crushed
½ teaspoon dried oregano
leaves, crushed
2 thinly sliced green onions
and tops *or* minced
parsley

Cook and stir onion and garlic in oil in medium skillet until tender; add spinach and cook over medium heat until mixture is very dry. In medium bowl, combine spinach mixture, cheeses, egg, sugar and pepper. Spread scant ½ cup mixture on each lasagna noodle and roll up, lengthwise. Place lasagna rolls seam-side down in greased 13 × 9-inch baking pan. Cover; bake in preheated 350°F oven until hot, about 20 minutes.

Heat tomato sauce, mushrooms and herbs in small saucepan. Spoon sauce onto serving plates. Cut lasagna rolls into thirds; place cut-sides up on sauce. Sprinkle with green onions.

Makes 6 servings

Favorite recipe from **Canned Food Information Council**

Spinach-Cheese Lasagna Rolls

Tomato Chicken Curry

1 pound boneless skinless chicken breasts, cut into bite-size cubes
2 tablespoons all-purpose flour
2 tablespoons vegetable oil
1 cup chopped onions
½ cup julienne-cut carrots
2 cloves garlic, minced
1 (8-ounce) can HUNT'S® Tomato Sauce
1 cup frozen peas
½ cup chicken broth
½ teaspoon *each* curry powder and salt
¼ teaspoon black pepper
Dash ground red pepper
½ pound uncooked linguine or fettuccine, cooked according to package directions and drained

In large plastic food bag, combine chicken and flour. Shake to coat chicken thoroughly. In large nonstick skillet, cook and stir chicken in oil until chicken just begins to brown; remove and set aside. In same saucepan, cook and stir onions, carrots and garlic until onions start to soften. Add cooked chicken and remaining ingredients except pasta; mix thoroughly. Simmer, uncovered, 5 minutes until sauce thickens. Serve over hot pasta.

Makes 4 to 6 servings

Three Cheese Macaroni

1½ cups uncooked elbow macaroni
3 tablespoons butter or margarine
3 tablespoons flour
½ teaspoon salt
Dash pepper
3 cups milk
1½ cups (6 ounces) SARGENTO® Shredded or Fancy Shredded Cheddar Cheese
1 cup (4 ounces) SARGENTO® Fancy Shredded Swiss Cheese
¼ cup (2 ounces) SARGENTO® Grated Cheese*
Additional SARGENTO® Grated Cheese, optional

Cook macaroni according to package directions; drain. In medium saucepan, melt butter. Stir in flour, salt and pepper. Gradually stir in milk. Cook and stir until thick and bubbly. Remove from heat. Add Cheddar and Swiss cheeses; stir until melted. Stir in Grated Cheese. Mix macaroni with cheese sauce. Pour into lightly greased 2-quart casserole. Sprinkle with additional Grated Cheese if desired. Bake uncovered at 350°F for 35 to 40 minutes or until top begins to brown.   *Makes 8 servings*

*SARGENTO® Parmesan, Parmesan and Romano or Italian-Style Grated Cheese may also be used.

Vegetable Stuffed Manicotti

6 PASTA DEFINO® No Boil® Lasagna Noodles
1¼ cups finely shredded zucchini
¾ cup finely shredded carrots
½ cup finely sliced green onions
1 cup ricotta cheese
1 egg, slightly beaten
12 ounces (3 cups) shredded mozzarella cheese, divided
2 cups prepared spaghetti sauce

Soak lasagna noodles in hot tap water for 5 to 8 minutes or until softened, taking care noodles do not stick together. In large bowl, combine vegetables, ricotta cheese, egg and 1½ cups mozzarella cheese; mix well. Cut each softened lasagna noodle in half, making two 4-inch squares. Spray 13 × 9 × 2-inch baking pan with nonstick cooking spray. Divide vegetable mixture equally among noodle squares; roll up. Place seam-side down in baking dish. Pour spaghetti sauce over tops of rolled noodles. Sprinkle with remaining 1½ cups mozzarella cheese. Cover with foil. Bake in 400°F oven for 15 minutes. Uncover; bake an additional 20 to 25 minutes, or until center is hot and cheese is bubbly.   *Makes 4 to 6 servings*

Seafood Lasagna

1 package (16 ounces) uncooked lasagna noodles
¾ teaspoon dried tarragon, crushed
3 cups prepared white sauce, homemade* or from package mix
1½ pounds seafood (any combination of shrimp, crabmeat, firm fish fillets or surimi seafood); cut into bite-size pieces
2 cups (8 ounces) SARGENTO® Preferred Light Fancy Supreme Shredded Mozzarella Cheese
¾ cup (3 ounces) SARGENTO® Fancy Shredded Parmesan Cheese**

Prepare lasagna noodles according to package directions; drain. Add tarragon to white sauce. In greased 13 × 9-inch baking dish, layer ⅓ noodles, ½ the seafood, ⅓ *each* mozzarella, Parmesan and white sauce; repeat. Top with remaining noodles, white sauce and cheeses. Bake in preheated 350°F oven for 30 minutes or until bubbly. Let stand 10 minutes before serving.
Makes 8 to 10 servings

*To prepare white sauce, melt 6 tablespoons butter or margarine in saucepan over low heat. Stir in 6 tablespoons flour; cook until well blended. Gradually add 3 cups milk, stirring constantly until smooth and thickened.

**Substitution: Use 1 cup (4 ounces) SARGENTO® Parmesan, Parmesan and Romano or Italian-Style Grated Cheese.

Layered Pasta Ricotta Pie

¼ (1-pound) package
    CREAMETTE® Vermicelli
⅓ cup finely chopped onion
4 cloves garlic, finely chopped
1 tablespoon olive or
    vegetable oil
1 cup grated fresh Romano
    cheese
3 eggs
1 (15- or 16-ounce) container
    ricotta cheese
1 (10-ounce) package frozen
    chopped spinach, thawed
    and *well drained*
½ teaspoon salt
1 (26-ounce) jar CLASSICO®
    Di Sicilia (Ripe Olives &
    Mushrooms) Pasta Sauce

Preheat oven to 350°. Break
vermicelli into thirds; cook
according to package directions.
Drain. Meanwhile, in large skillet,
cook onion and garlic in oil until
tender; remove from heat. Add
cooked vermicelli, *½ cup*
Romano cheese and *1 egg;* mix
well. Press into well-greased 9-
inch springform pan. Combine *2
egg yolks,* ricotta, spinach, salt
and remaining *½ cup* Romano
cheese. Spread over pasta layer.
In small mixer bowl, beat *2 egg
whites* until stiff but not dry; fold
into *1½ cups* pasta sauce. Pour
over spinach mixture. Bake 50 to
60 minutes or until set; let stand
10 minutes. Heat remaining pasta
sauce; serve with pie. Garnish as
desired. Refrigerate leftovers.

Makes 6 to 8 servings

Tuna Stuffed Shells

12 uncooked jumbo shell
    macaroni
1 can (6½ ounces) tuna,
    drained, flaked
⅔ cup ricotta cheese
1 egg, well beaten
½ cup HEINZ® Seafood Cocktail
    Sauce
⅓ cup chopped red bell
    pepper
¼ cup sliced green onions
¼ cup finely chopped celery
2 tablespoons dry bread
    crumbs
2 tablespoons grated
    Parmesan cheese
⅛ to ¼ teaspoon hot pepper
    sauce
2 tablespoons water
½ cup (2 ounces) shredded
    mozzarella cheese
    Additional HEINZ® Seafood
    Cocktail Sauce

Cook shells according to
package directions; drain.
Combine tuna, ricotta cheese,
egg, ½ cup Cocktail Sauce,
vegetables, bread crumbs,
Parmesan and hot pepper sauce;
stuff into shells. Arrange shells in
1½-quart baking dish. Add water
to dish; cover tightly with foil.
Bake in 375°F oven for 35 minutes.
Top with mozzarella cheese.
Bake, uncovered, 2 minutes or
until cheese is melted. Let stand 5
minutes. Serve with additional
Seafood Cocktail Sauce.

Makes 4 servings

Layered Pasta Ricotta Pie

Pasta & Veal Naples Style

Pasta & Veal Naples Style

½ (1-pound) package
    CREAMETTE® Linguine,
    cooked according to
    package directions and
    drained
2 eggs
2 tablespoons water
½ teaspoon garlic salt
8 thin veal cutlets (about
    1 pound)
2 cups plain dry bread crumbs
½ cup butter or margarine
2 tablespoons olive oil
1 (26-ounce) jar CLASSICO®
    Di Napoli (Tomato & Basil)
    or Di Parma (Four Cheese)
    or Di Sicilia (Ripe Olives &
    Mushrooms) Pasta Sauce
Grated Parmesan cheese or
    shredded mozzarella
    cheese

In medium bowl, beat eggs, water and garlic salt. Dip veal in crumbs then in egg mixture and again in crumbs. In large skillet, over medium heat, melt butter with oil; brown veal on both sides until cooked through. In medium saucepan, heat pasta sauce. Arrange veal on hot cooked linguine; top with pasta sauce. Garnish with cheese. Refrigerate leftovers.   *Makes 4 servings*

Chicken Stroganoff

2 pounds boneless chicken breasts, skinned and cut into thin strips
½ cup all-purpose flour
1½ teaspoons salt
⅛ teaspoon pepper
⅓ cup plus 3 tablespoons CRISCO® Shortening
½ cup finely chopped onion
2 cups chicken broth
½ pound fresh mushrooms, cleaned and sliced
¾ cup sour cream
3 tablespoons tomato paste
1 teaspoon Worcestershire sauce
Buttered noodles

Coat chicken strips evenly with mixture of flour, salt and pepper.

Melt ⅓ cup CRISCO® in large heavy skillet. Add chicken strips and onion; cook and stir until chicken is evenly browned on all sides. Add broth; cover. Simmer about 20 minutes or until meat is tender. Remove from heat.

Melt 3 tablespoons CRISCO® in small skillet over medium heat. Add mushrooms; cook and stir until lightly browned and tender. Add to chicken mixture.

Combine sour cream, tomato paste and Worcestershire sauce; add in small amounts to chicken mixture, stirring until well combined.

Return to heat. Cook and stir over low heat until hot. Serve with buttered noodles.

Makes 8 servings

Easy Macaroni and Cheese

1 (46-fluid ounce) can COLLEGE INN® Chicken or Beef Broth
1 (12-ounce) package uncooked spiral macaroni
½ cup BLUE BONNET® Margarine, divided
¼ cup all-purpose flour
2 cups (8 ounces) shredded Cheddar cheese
30 RITZ® Crackers, coarsely crushed

In large heavy saucepan, heat broth to a boil; add macaroni and cook according to package directions, omitting salt. Drain, reserving 2 cups broth (if necessary, add water). Set aside.

In medium saucepan, over medium-high heat, melt ¼ cup margarine. Blend in flour. Gradually add reserved broth, stirring constantly until mixture thickens and boils. Cook and stir 2 minutes. Stir in cheese until melted. Combine cheese sauce and macaroni in 2-quart casserole. Melt remaining ¼ cup margarine; stir in cracker crumbs. Sprinkle over macaroni mixture. Bake at 400°F for 30 minutes or until hot.

Makes 6 to 8 servings

Cheesy Chicken Tetrazzini

2 whole chicken breasts, boned, skinned and cut into 1-inch pieces
2 tablespoons butter or margarine
1½ cups sliced mushrooms
1 small red bell pepper, cut into julienne strips
½ cup sliced green onions
¼ cup unsifted all-purpose flour
1¾ cups chicken broth
1 cup light cream or half-and-half
2 tablespoons dry sherry
½ teaspoon salt
¼ teaspoon black pepper
¼ teaspoon dried thyme, crushed
1 package (8 ounces) uncooked tri-color rotelle pasta, cooked until just tender and drained
¼ cup grated Parmesan cheese
2 tablespoons chopped parsley
1 cup (4 ounces) shredded nokkelost or Jarlsberg cheese

In large skillet, brown chicken in butter. Add mushrooms; cook and stir until brown. Add red bell pepper and green onions. Cook several minutes, stirring occasionally, until tender. Stir in flour; cook and stir several minutes until blended. Gradually blend in chicken broth, cream and sherry. Cook, stirring, until thickened and smooth. Season with salt, black pepper and thyme. Toss sauce mixture with pasta, Parmesan cheese and parsley. Spoon into 1½ quart baking dish. Bake at 350°F for 30 minutes. Top with shredded cheese. Bake until cheese is melted. *Makes 6 servings*

Favorite recipe from Norseland Foods

Speedy Stroganoff

1 pound beef sirloin, cut into narrow strips
1 tablespoon CRISCO® Shortening
1 medium onion, sliced
1 clove garlic, minced
1 can (10¾ ounces) condensed cream of mushroom soup
1 cup sour cream
1 can (4 ounces) sliced mushrooms, undrained
2 tablespoons ketchup
2 teaspoons Worcestershire sauce
Poppy Noodles (recipe follows)

In large skillet, brown beef strips in hot CRISCO®. Add onion and garlic; cook until onion is crisp-tender. Combine soup, sour cream, mushrooms with liquid, ketchup and Worcestershire; pour over beef mixture. Cook and stir over low heat until hot. Serve over Poppy Noodles.

Makes 4 servings

Poppy Noodles
Toss 4 cups hot cooked noodles with 1 tablespoon butter and 1 teaspoon poppy seed.

Smoked Sausage Noodle Bake

8 ounces uncooked medium egg noodles
2 tablespoons butter or margarine
½ cup chopped onion
½ cup chopped celery
1 can (17 ounces) cream-style corn
½ cup sour cream
½ teaspoon salt
Dash ground black pepper
1 pound ECKRICH® Smoked Sausage

Preheat oven to 350°F. Cook noodles according to package directions; drain. Melt butter in small saucepan over medium-high heat. Cook and stir onion and celery until crisp-tender. Combine noodles, onion mixture, corn, sour cream, salt and pepper in large bowl. Pour into buttered shallow 2-quart baking dish. Cut sausage into serving-size pieces. Arrange on top of noodles; push down partially into noodles. Bake 40 minutes or until hot.

Makes 4 to 6 servings

Zucchini Pasta Bake

Prep and Cook time: 33 minutes

1½ cups uncooked pasta tubes
½ pound ground beef
½ cup chopped onion
1 clove garlic, minced
Salt and pepper
1 teaspoon dried basil, crushed
1 can (16 ounces) DEL MONTE® Zucchini with Italian-Style Tomato Sauce
1 cup (4 ounces) shredded Monterey Jack cheese

Cook pasta according to package directions; drain. In large skillet, cook beef with onion and garlic; drain. Season with salt and pepper. Stir in basil and zucchini with tomato sauce. Place pasta in 8-inch square baking dish. Top with meat mixture. Bake at 350°F for 15 minutes. Top with cheese. Bake 3 minutes or until cheese is melted.

Makes 4 servings

Chicken Roman Style

2½ to 3 pounds chicken pieces
¼ cup olive oil
3 ounces prosciutto or cooked ham, thinly sliced and cut into strips
1 (26-ounce) jar CLASSICO® Di Roma Arrabbiata (Spicy Red Pepper) *or* Di Salerno (Sweet Peppers & Onions) Pasta Sauce
¼ cup dry white wine
½ (1-pound) package CREAMETTE® Fettuccini, cooked according to package directions and drained

In large skillet, brown chicken in oil. Remove chicken; pour off oil. In same skillet, over medium-high heat, cook prosciutto until lightly browned. Reduce heat; stir in pasta sauce and wine. Return chicken to skillet; cover and simmer 20 minutes or until chicken is tender. Serve chicken and sauce over hot cooked fettuccini. Refrigerate leftovers.

Makes 4 to 6 servings

Fiesta Chicken Breasts

12 ounces uncooked spinach fettuccine or linguine
3 tablespoons butter or margarine
3 whole chicken breasts, split, boned and skinned
1 jar (7 ounces) roasted red peppers, drained and sliced into 1/2-inch strips (1 cup)
1/4 cup sliced green onions
1/4 cup flour
1 cup chicken broth
1 cup milk
1/4 cup dry white wine
1 1/2 cups (6 ounces) SARGENTO® Shredded Monterey Jack or Mild Cheddar Cheese
1/4 cup coarsely chopped fresh cilantro

Cook fettuccine according to package directions. Drain well and transfer to serving platter; keep warm. Meanwhile, melt butter in large skillet over medium heat. Add chicken; cook until golden brown and cooked through, about 5 minutes per side. Place chicken over fettuccine. Top with red pepper strips; keep warm. Add green onions to drippings in skillet; cook 1 minute. Add flour; cook 1 minute, stirring constantly. Add broth, milk and wine; bring to a boil and cook until thickened, stirring constantly. Add Monterey Jack cheese; stir until melted. Pour evenly over chicken, peppers and fettuccine; sprinkle with cilantro.

Makes 6 servings

Tomato Pesto Lasagna

Prep time: 20 minutes
Bake time: 30 minutes

8 ounces uncooked lasagna noodles
1 pound sausage or ground beef
1 can (14 1/2 ounces) DEL MONTE® Chunky Pasta Recipe Stewed Tomatoes, undrained
1 can (6 ounces) DEL MONTE® Tomato Paste
3/4 cup water
8 ounces ricotta cheese
1 package (4 ounces) frozen pesto, thawed
8 ounces (2 cups) shredded mozzarella cheese

Cook noodles according to package directions; rinse, drain and separate noodles. Brown meat in 10-inch skillet; drain. Stir in tomatoes with juice, tomato paste and water; mix well. In 2-quart or 9-inch square baking dish, layer 1/3 meat sauce, half each of noodles, ricotta cheese, pesto and mozzarella cheese; repeat layers ending with meat sauce. Bake at 350°F for 30 minutes or until heated through.

Makes 6 servings

To Microwave: Prepare lasagna noodles as directed above. In 9-inch square microwavable dish, assemble lasagna as directed above. Cover with plastic wrap; cook on high (100% power) 10 minutes, rotating dish after 5 minutes.

Fiesta Chicken Breasts

Hearty Manicotti

Hearty Manicotti

- 1¼ cups water, divided
- 1 pound sweet (mild) Italian sausage links
- 1 pound ground beef
- 1 medium onion, chopped
- 1 can (15 ounces) tomato purée
- 1 can (6 ounces) tomato paste
- 1 teaspoon sugar
- ½ teaspoon black pepper
- 1¾ teaspoons dried basil, crushed, divided
- 1½ teaspoons salt, divided
- 1 package (12 ounces) manicotti shells
- 2 cups (15 ounces) SARGENTO® Ricotta Cheese*
- 2 cups (8 ounces) SARGENTO® Preferred Light Fancy Supreme Shredded Mozzarella Cheese, divided
- 2 tablespoons chopped parsley
- SARGENTO® Grated Cheese, optional**

In 5-quart covered Dutch oven, combine ¼ cup water and sausage; cook over medium heat 5 minutes. Uncover and allow sausage to brown well; drain sausage on paper towels.

Brown beef and onion in Dutch oven over medium heat; drain. Stir in tomato purée, tomato paste, sugar, pepper, 1 teaspoon basil, 1 teaspoon salt and remaining 1 cup water; cover and simmer 45 minutes.

Cut sausage into bite-size pieces; add to beef mixture. Simmer 15 minutes, stirring occasionally.

Meanwhile, cook manicotti shells according to package directions; rinse and drain well.

In large bowl, combine ricotta cheese, 1 cup mozzarella cheese, parsley, remaining ¾ teaspoon basil and remaining ½ teaspoon salt. Spoon into shells; set aside.

Spoon half of meat sauce into large shallow baking dish. Arrange cheese-stuffed shells over sauce. Spoon remaining sauce over shells. Sprinkle with remaining 1 cup mozzarella cheese. Bake in 375°F oven 30 minutes. Serve with Grated Cheese, if desired.

Makes 6 servings

*SARGENTO® Part-Skim Ricotta or Lite Ricotta can also be used.

**SARGENTO® Parmesan, Parmesan and Romano or Italian-Style Grated Cheese can also be used.

Quick Chicken Cacciatore

4 boneless skinless chicken
     breast halves (about
     1 pound)
   Salt and pepper
   Flour
2 cloves garlic, finely chopped
4 tablespoons olive oil
1 (26-ounce) jar CLASSICO®
     Di Napoli (Tomato & Basil)
     or Di Sicilia (Ripe Olives &
     Mushrooms) Pasta Sauce
1 small green bell pepper, cut
     into strips
1 small red bell pepper, cut
     into strips
2 slices Provolone cheese, cut
     in half
1 (7-ounce) package *or* 2 cups
     uncooked CREAMETTES®
     Elbow Macaroni, cooked
     according to package
     directions and drained
   Chopped parsley

Season chicken with salt and pepper; coat with flour. In large skillet, brown chicken and garlic in *3 tablespoons* oil; remove chicken from pan. Add pasta sauce then chicken. Bring to a boil; reduce heat. Cover and simmer 20 minutes, adding peppers during last 5 minutes. Uncover; top each chicken breast with half cheese slice. Toss hot cooked macaroni with remaining *1 tablespoon* oil and parsley. Serve with chicken and sauce. Refrigerate leftovers.

Makes 4 servings

Quick Chicken Cacciatore

Manicotti Villa Santa Maria

1 (15- or 16-ounce) container ricotta cheese
1½ cups (6 ounces) shredded mozzarella cheese
4 ounces prosciutto or cooked ham, thinly sliced and finely chopped, optional
2 eggs, beaten
¼ cup chopped parsley
⅛ teaspoon pepper
½ cup grated Parmesan cheese
½ (1-pound) package CREAMETTE® Manicotti, cooked according to package directions and drained
1 (26-ounce) jar CLASSICO® D'Abruzzi (Beef & Pork) *or* Di Salerno (Sweet Peppers & Onions) Pasta Sauce

Preheat oven to 375°. In large bowl, combine ricotta and mozzarella cheese, prosciutto if desired, eggs, parsley, pepper and ¼ *cup* Parmesan cheese; mix well. Stuff manicotti with cheese mixture; arrange in 13 × 9-inch baking dish. Spoon pasta sauce over manicotti; top with remaining ¼ *cup* Parmesan cheese. Cover; bake 40 minutes or until hot. Refrigerate leftovers.

Makes 6 to 8 servings

Pesto Lasagna Rolls

2 cups fresh basil leaves
2 cloves garlic
1 cup (3 ounces) SARGENTO® Fancy Shredded Parmesan Cheese, divided
¾ cup olive oil
1 container (15 ounces) SARGENTO® Ricotta Cheese*
1 cup (4 ounces) SARGENTO® Preferred Light Fancy Supreme Shredded Mozzarella Cheese
1 egg, beaten
1 cup diced zucchini
16 lasagna noodles, cooked, drained and cooled

Prepare pesto sauce in covered blender or food processor by processing basil with garlic until chopped. Add ½ cup Parmesan cheese; process until well mixed. With machine running, slowly add oil and continue processing until smooth. Set aside. In medium bowl, combine ricotta and mozzarella cheese, remaining ½ cup Parmesan cheese and egg; blend well. Fold in zucchini. Spread 2 heaping tablespoons cheese mixture on each lasagna noodle. Roll up each noodle lengthwise and stand vertically in greased 11 × 7-inch baking dish. Pour pesto sauce over lasagna rolls; cover and bake in preheated 350°F oven 40 minutes or until bubbly and heated through. *Makes 8 servings*

*SARGENTO® Part-Skim Ricotta or Lite Ricotta can also be used.

Chicken Marsala

5 boneless chicken breast
    fillets
¼ cup all-purpose flour
½ teaspoon salt
¼ teaspoon pepper
2 tablespoons vegetable oil
2 cups sliced mushrooms
1 clove garlic, minced
1 (14½-ounce) can HUNT'S®
    Whole Tomatoes, drained
    and chopped
1 (8-ounce) can HUNT'S®
    Tomato Sauce
⅓ cup Marsala wine
½ teaspoon dried basil,
    crumbled
1 pound uncooked linguine,
    cooked according to
    package directions and
    drained

In large plastic food bag, combine chicken, flour, salt and pepper. Shake to coat chicken thoroughly. In large skillet, brown chicken in oil 5 minutes on each side; remove and set aside. In same skillet, cook and stir mushrooms and garlic 2 to 3 minutes. Stir in tomatoes, tomato sauce, wine and basil; simmer 1 to 2 minutes. Return chicken to pan; mix with sauce. Cover; simmer 5 minutes, turning chicken once during cooking. Serve over hot linguine.

Makes 5 servings

Veal 'n' Spaghetti Casserole

Casserole

1½ pounds boneless veal
    shoulder, cut into 1-inch
    cubes
¾ cup chopped onion
1 teaspoon salt
½ teaspoon pepper
2 cups water
1 package (7 ounces)
    uncooked thin spaghetti,
    hot cooked and drained
1 can (6 ounces) sliced
    mushrooms, undrained
1 cup sour cream

Topping

3 tablespoons CRISCO®
    Shortening
1 cup fresh bread crumbs
½ cup grated Parmesan
    cheese
½ cup snipped parsley

Place veal, onion, salt, pepper and water in Dutch oven. Bring to a boil. Reduce heat to low; simmer, covered, until meat is tender (about 30 minutes).

Preheat oven to 350°F. Mix cooked spaghetti, undrained mushrooms and sour cream into veal mixture. Turn into greased 2½-quart casserole.

For Topping, melt CRISCO® in small skillet; stir in bread crumbs. Remove from heat; stir in cheese and parsley. Sprinkle over veal mixture.

Bake, uncovered, for 35 to 40 minutes or until mixture is bubbly and crumb topping is golden brown. *Makes 8 servings*

Beef 'n Eggplant Stir-Fry

Prep time: 35 minutes
Cook time: 25 to 30 minutes

1 beef flank steak (1 to
   1¼ pounds)
4 tablespoons dry red wine,
   divided
½ teaspoon dried basil leaves,
   crushed
½ teaspoon dried oregano
   leaves, crushed
½ teaspoon salt
¼ teaspoon black pepper
1 eggplant (approximately
   1 pound), pared, cut into
   2 × ¼-inch strips
2 cloves garlic, minced
4 to 5 tablespoons olive oil,
   divided
1 large red bell pepper, cut
   into thin strips
1 tablespoon cornstarch
¾ cup beef broth
2 cups cooked and drained
   spinach linguini
1 tablespoon grated Parmesan
   cheese

Partially freeze beef flank steak to firm. Cut steak in half lengthwise; slice each half diagonally across the grain into thin slices (knife should be almost parallel to cutting surface). Combine 1 tablespoon wine, basil, oregano, salt and black pepper; sprinkle over meat. Stir-fry eggplant and garlic in 3 tablespoons hot oil in wok or large nonstick skillet 8 to 10 minutes or until eggplant is transparent. Add red bell pepper; continue cooking 2 minutes.

Remove from wok; reserve. Stir-fry beef strips (⅓ at a time) in remaining oil 2 to 3 minutes. Remove from wok; reserve. Combine cornstarch with beef broth. Stir into drippings in wok with remaining 3 tablespoons wine. Cook until thickened, stirring occasionally. Stir in reserved beef strips and vegetable mixture; heat through. Combine hot linguini with Parmesan cheese. Serve stir-fry mixture over linguini.

Makes 4 servings

Favorite recipe from **National Live Stock and Meat Board**

Quick Chili Bake

1 can (15 to 16 ounces) chili
1 jar (12 ounces) mild or
   medium chunky salsa
1 can (12 ounces) corn,
   drained
7 ounces uncooked
   MUELLER'S® Pasta Swirls,
   cooked 5 minutes and
   drained
½ cup (2 ounces) shredded
   Cheddar cheese

In large bowl, combine chili, salsa and corn. Add pasta; toss to coat. Spoon into 2-quart casserole; top with cheese. Bake in 400°F oven for 30 minutes or until heated. If desired, serve with corn chips.

Makes 6 servings

To Microwave: Prepare pasta mixture as directed; spoon into 2-quart microwavable casserole. Microwave at High (100% power) 15 minutes or until heated. Top with cheese. Microwave at High 1 minute or until cheese melts.

Beef 'n Eggplant Stir-Fry

Shells Florentine

Prep time: 30 minutes
Bake time: 35 minutes

1 cup coarsely chopped mushrooms (about 4 ounces)
½ cup chopped onion
1 clove garlic, minced
1 teaspoon Italian seasoning
¼ teaspoon ground black pepper
2 tablespoons FLEISCHMANN'S® Margarine
1 (16-ounce) container low-sodium lowfat cottage cheese (1% milkfat)
1 (10-ounce) package frozen chopped spinach, thawed and well drained
6 tablespoons EGG BEATERS® 99% Real Egg Product
24 jumbo shell macaroni, cooked in unsalted water and drained
1 (15¼-ounce) jar spaghetti sauce, divided

In large skillet, over medium-high heat, cook and stir mushrooms, onion, garlic, Italian seasoning and pepper in margarine until vegetables are tender, about 4 minutes. Remove from heat; stir in cottage cheese, spinach and egg product. Spoon mixture into shells.

Spread ½ cup spaghetti sauce in bottom of 13 × 9 × 2-inch baking dish; arrange shells over sauce. Top with remaining sauce; cover. Bake at 350°F for 35 minutes or until hot.　　*Makes 8 servings*

To Microwave: In 1½-quart microwavable bowl, combine mushrooms, onion, garlic, Italian seasoning, black pepper and margarine; cover. Microwave at HIGH (100% power) for 2 to 3 minutes or until vegetables are tender. Assemble shells as directed; spread ½ cup spaghetti sauce in bottom of 12 × 8 × 2-inch microwavable dish. Arrange shells over sauce. Top with remaining sauce; cover with plastic wrap, venting corner. Microwave at HIGH for 8 to 10 minutes or until hot. Let stand 5 minutes before serving.

Skillet Chili Olé

1 pound ground beef
1 small onion, chopped
½ teaspoon chili powder
1 can (4 ounces) chopped green chilies, drained (reserve liquid)
2⅓ cups water
1 package LIPTON® Pasta & Sauce — Herb Tomato
1 cup shredded Monterey Jack cheese (about 3 ounces)

In medium skillet, brown ground beef; drain. Combine onion and chili powder with reserved green chili liquid and water. Add to ground beef; bring to a boil. Stir in pasta & herb tomato sauce; continue boiling over medium heat, stirring occasionally, 8 minutes or until pasta is tender. Remove from heat. Stir in chilies and sprinkle with cheese; let stand, covered, 5 minutes or until cheese melts.

Makes about 4 servings

Skillet Pasta Roma

Skillet Pasta Roma

Prep time: 15 minutes
Cook time: 30 minutes

½ **pound Italian sausage,**
sliced or crumbled
1 **large onion, coarsely**
chopped
1 **large clove garlic, minced**
2 **cans (14½ ounces each)**
DEL MONTE® Chunky Pasta
Recipe Stewed Tomatoes,
undrained
1 **can (8 ounces) DEL MONTE®**
Tomato Sauce
1 **cup water**
8 **ounces uncooked rigatoni**
or spiral pasta
8 **sliced mushrooms, optional**
Grated Parmesan cheese
and parsley, optional

In large skillet, brown sausage. Add onion and garlic. Cook until onion is soft; drain. Stir in stewed tomatoes with juice, tomato sauce, water and pasta. Cover and bring to a boil; reduce heat. Simmer, covered, 25 to 30 minutes or until pasta is tender, stirring occasionally. Stir in mushrooms; simmer 5 minutes. Serve in skillet garnished with cheese and parsley, if desired.

Makes 4 servings

Turkey Stuffed Pasta Italiano

- 1 pound ground California Turkey
- 1 cup minced onion
- 1 cup grated, peeled eggplant
- 2 cloves garlic, minced
  Salt and pepper
- 1 can (28 ounces) tomatoes, undrained
- 1 can (8 ounces) tomato sauce
- 1 cup red wine or water
- 1 teaspoon garlic salt
- 1 teaspoon dried oregano, crushed
- 1 teaspoon dried basil, crushed
- ½ teaspoon dried tarragon, crushed
- ½ teaspoon crushed red pepper
- 1 package (12 ounces) uncooked jumbo pasta shells
- ½ cup grated Parmesan cheese
- ¾ cup (3 ounces) shredded mozzarella cheese

In large non-stick skillet, brown turkey, onion, eggplant and garlic until turkey is no longer pink; drain. Season with salt and pepper; reserve. In small saucepan, simmer tomatoes with juice, tomato sauce, wine and seasonings for 15 minutes. Cook pasta shells until done, but still firm; drain. In large bowl, combine turkey mixture and Parmesan cheese with half the tomato sauce mixture. Stuff shells; place in 13 × 9-inch pan. Spoon remaining sauce mixture over shells; top with mozzarella cheese. Bake at 350°F for 30 minutes.

Makes 8 to 10 servings

Note: Shells can be stuffed ahead of time and refrigerated. Add sauce and mozzarella cheese just before baking. Increase cooking time by 8 to 10 minutes.

Favorite recipe from **California Poultry Industry Federation**

Chile Cheese Macaroni

- 8 ounces uncooked elbow macaroni, cooked and drained
- 2 cups (8 ounces) shredded processed American cheese
- 2 (4-ounce) cans or 1 (7-ounce) can ORTEGA® Diced Green Chiles, undrained
- ¼ cup milk
- ⅛ teaspoon ground black pepper
- ¼ cup chopped parsley, optional

In large bowl, combine macaroni, cheese, chiles, milk and pepper. Spoon into greased 1½-quart casserole; cover. Bake at 350°F for 45 minutes or until hot. Garnish with parsley if desired.

Makes 4 (1-cup) servings

Turkey Stuffed Pasta Italiano

Turkey Rolls Di Napoli

1 green bell pepper, cut into strips
1 red bell pepper, cut into strips
1 clove garlic, finely chopped
3 tablespoons olive oil
6 (4-ounce) fresh turkey breast slices, pounded and lightly seasoned with salt and pepper
3 ounces Swiss cheese, cut into 12 strips
1 (26-ounce) jar CLASSICO® Di Napoli (Tomato & Basil) Pasta Sauce
½ (1-pound) package CREAMETTE® Linguine or Rotini, cooked according to package directions and drained

In large skillet, cook peppers and garlic in *2 tablespoons* oil until tender; remove from pan. On each turkey cutlet, place one green and one red bell pepper strip and 2 cheese strips. Roll tightly and secure with wooden picks. In same skillet, heat remaining *1 tablespoon* oil. Over medium-high heat, brown turkey rolls. Add pasta sauce and remaining bell peppers. Reduce heat; cover and simmer 10 minutes or until hot. Remove picks; serve over hot cooked pasta. Refrigerate leftovers.

Makes 4 to 6 servings

Jarlsberg Pasta Pie

3 cups cooked thin spaghetti
1½ cups shredded Jarlsberg cheese, divided
1 egg, slightly beaten
1 pound ground beef
2 cups sliced zucchini
1 cup chopped onion
1 medium clove garlic, minced
1 teaspoon dried basil, crushed
1 can (16 ounces) stewed tomatoes, undrained
1 can (8 ounces) tomato sauce

In large bowl, blend pasta, 1 cup cheese and egg. Line bottom and sides of 10-inch pie plate with mixture; set aside. In large skillet, brown beef; pour off fat. Add zucchini, onion, garlic and basil; cook until vegetables are tender. Blend in tomatoes with juice and tomato sauce. Spoon into pasta mixture in pie plate. Bake at 350°F for 30 minutes. Sprinkle with remaining ½ cup cheese. Bake an additional 10 minutes.

Makes 6 to 8 servings

Favorite recipe from **Norseland Foods, Inc.**

TOPPERS & TOSS-INS

Pasta & Vegetable Toss

½ cup chopped onion
1 clove garlic, finely chopped
1 teaspoon Italian seasoning
1 tablespoon olive oil
¼ cup water
2 teaspoons WYLER'S® or STEERO® Beef-Flavor Instant Bouillon
2 cups broccoli flowerets
2 cups sliced zucchini
8 ounces fresh mushrooms, sliced (about 2 cups)
1 medium red bell pepper, cut into thin strips
½ (1-pound) package CREAMETTE® Fettuccini, cooked according to package directions and drained

In large skillet, cook onion, garlic and Italian seasoning in oil until tender. Add water, bouillon and vegetables. Cover and simmer 5 to 7 minutes until vegetables are tender-crisp. Toss with hot fettuccini. Serve immediately. Refrigerate leftovers.

Makes 4 servings

Pasta Delight

1 medium zucchini, sliced
1 tablespoon olive oil
2 tablespoons chopped shallots
2 cloves garlic, chopped
1 medium tomato, diced
2 tablespoons chopped fresh basil *or* ½ teaspoon dried basil, crushed
2 tablespoons grated Parmesan cheese
12 ounces uncooked penne pasta, hot cooked and drained

Cook and stir zucchini in hot oil in large skillet over medium-high heat. Reduce heat to medium. Add shallots and garlic; cook 1 minute. Add tomato; cook and stir 45 seconds. Add basil and cheese. Pour vegetable mixture over penne in large bowl; toss gently to mix.

Makes 4 to 6 servings

Favorite recipe from **National Pasta Association**

Pasta & Vegetable Toss

Picante Pesto Linguine

1⅔ cups firmly packed fresh
　　spinach leaves
¾ cup PACE® Picante Sauce,
　　divided
⅔ cup grated Parmesan
　　cheese
½ cup pecans, coarsely
　　chopped
⅓ cup vegetable oil
1 clove garlic, chopped
1 pound uncooked linguine or
　　other favorite pasta, hot
　　cooked and drained
　　Additional chopped pecans,
　　optional
　　Additional PACE® Picante
　　Sauce, optional

Combine spinach, ¼ cup
picante sauce, cheese, ½ cup
pecans, oil and garlic in covered
food processor or blender
container; process until smooth.
Transfer to small bowl; stir in
remaining ½ cup picante sauce.
Toss spinach mixture with hot
cooked pasta in large bowl.
Sprinkle with additional chopped
pecans and serve with additional
picante sauce, if desired.

Makes 4 to 6 servings

Picante Pesto Linguine

Pasta Ratatouille

1 medium onion, halved and
　　thinly sliced
2 cloves garlic, minced
2 tablespoons vegetable oil
1 small eggplant (1 pound),
　　peeled, cut into ½-inch
　　cubes
2 medium zucchini, halved
　　lengthwise, cut into ¼-inch
　　slices
2 cans (16 ounces each)
　　tomatoes, undrained, cut
　　into bite-size pieces
¼ cup HEINZ® Worcestershire
　　Sauce
1½ teaspoons Italian seasoning
¼ teaspoon pepper
8 ounces uncooked linguine
½ cup grated Parmesan
　　cheese
　　Additional Parmesan cheese,
　　optional

In large skillet, cook and stir onion
and garlic in oil until onion is
tender. Stir in eggplant, zucchini,
tomatoes with juice,
Worcestershire sauce, Italian
seasoning and pepper. Simmer,
covered, 20 minutes, stirring
occasionally. Meanwhile, cook
linguine according to package
directions; drain. In large bowl,
toss linguine with vegetable
mixture and ½ cup Parmesan
cheese. Let stand 5 minutes
before serving. Serve with
additional Parmesan cheese, if
desired.　　*Makes 4 to 6 servings*

Tortellini Primavera

Tortellini Primavera

Prep time: 10 minutes
Cook time: 10 minutes

1 cup sliced mushrooms
½ cup chopped onion
1 clove garlic, minced
2 tablespoons PARKAY®
    Margarine
1 package (10 ounces)
    BIRDS EYE® Chopped
    Spinach, thawed, well
    drained
1 container (8 ounces)
    PHILADELPHIA BRAND® Soft
    Cream Cheese
1 medium tomato, chopped
¼ cup milk
¼ cup (1 ounce) KRAFT®
    100% Grated Parmesan
    Cheese
1 teaspoon Italian seasoning
¼ teaspoon salt
¼ teaspoon pepper
8 to 9 ounces fresh or frozen
    cheese-filled tortellini,
    cooked and drained

Cook and stir mushrooms, onion and garlic in margarine in large skillet. Add remaining ingredients except tortellini; mix well. Cook until mixture just begins to boil, stirring occasionally. Stir in tortellini; cook until thoroughly heated. **Makes 4 servings**

Creamy Fettuccine Alfredo

1 (8-ounce) package
   PHILADELPHIA BRAND®
   Cream Cheese, cubed
¾ cup (3 ounces) KRAFT®
   100% Grated Parmesan
   Cheese
½ cup PARKAY® Margarine
½ cup milk
8 ounces uncooked fettuccine,
   hot cooked and drained

In large saucepan, combine cream cheese, Parmesan cheese, margarine and milk; stir over low heat until smooth. Add fettuccine; toss lightly.

Makes 4 servings

Peppery Pasta Toss

1 cup FLEISCHMANN'S® Extra
   Light Margarine
1 tablespoon dry sherry
2 cloves garlic, minced
½ teaspoon dried oregano,
   crushed
½ teaspoon dried basil,
   crushed
¼ teaspoon coarsely ground
   black pepper
¼ teaspoon crushed red
   pepper
1 pound cooked pasta

In small saucepan, melt margarine. Add sherry, garlic, oregano, basil, black pepper and red pepper. Bring mixture to a boil. Reduce heat to low; simmer 10 minutes. Serve over cooked pasta. *Makes 8 servings*

Pasta with Spinach-Cheese Sauce

¼ cup FILIPPO BERIO® Extra-
   Virgin Flavorful Olive Oil,
   divided
1 medium onion, chopped
1 clove garlic, chopped
3 cups chopped fresh spinach,
   washed and well drained
1 cup lowfat ricotta or cottage
   cheese
½ cup chopped fresh parsley
1 teaspoon dried basil leaves,
   crushed
1 teaspoon lemon juice
¼ teaspoon black pepper
¼ teaspoon ground nutmeg
¾ pound uncooked spaghetti

1. Heat 3 tablespoons olive oil in large skillet over medium heat. Cook and stir onion and garlic until onion is tender.

2. Add spinach to skillet; cook 3 to 5 minutes or until spinach wilts.

3. Place spinach mixture, cheese, parsley, basil, lemon juice, pepper and nutmeg in covered blender container. Blend until smooth. Leave in blender, covered, to keep sauce warm.

4. Cook pasta according to package directions. Do not overcook. Drain pasta, reserving ¼ cup water. In large bowl, toss pasta with remaining 1 tablespoon olive oil.

5. Add reserved ¼ cup water to sauce in blender. Blend; serve over pasta. *Makes 4 servings*

Bacon and Creamy Herb Noodles

- 1 package (12 ounces) LOUIS RICH® Turkey Bacon, cut into ½-inch pieces
- 8 ounces fresh mushrooms, sliced
- 6 green onions with tops, sliced
- 8 ounces uncooked medium egg noodles
- 1 package (8 ounces) Neufchatel or light cream cheese, cubed
- ⅓ cup *each* white wine and water *or* ⅔ cup skim milk
- ½ teaspoon *each* garlic powder, dried basil and dried thyme leaves
- 1 small tomato, chopped

Heat Turkey Bacon in nonstick skillet over medium heat about 10 minutes or until lightly browned, stirring frequently. Add mushrooms and onions; cook and stir an additional 4 minutes. Reserve. Meanwhile, cook noodles according to package directions in large saucepan or Dutch oven; drain. Return noodles to saucepan; add remaining ingredients except tomato. Cook and stir over medium heat until cheese melts and sauce is well blended. Add reserved Turkey Bacon mixture; toss to combine. Sprinkle with tomato before serving. Garnish as desired.

Makes 8 servings

Easy Pasta Primavera

- 1 eggplant, peeled and cut into small sticks
- ½ pound fresh mushrooms, sliced
- 2 medium carrots, peeled and sliced diagonally
- 3 to 5 cloves fresh garlic, minced
- 3 tablespoons olive oil
- 2 medium zucchini, shredded
- 1 teaspoon dried oregano, crushed
- 1 teaspoon dried basil, crushed
- 1 large tomato, cut into wedges
- 2 tablespoons water
- 12 ounces uncooked spaghetti or other thin pasta, hot cooked and drained
- Grated Romano cheese

In large skillet, stir-fry eggplant, mushrooms, carrots and garlic in oil over high heat for 2 minutes. Stir in zucchini, oregano and basil; stir-fry 1 minute more. Add tomato wedges and water; cover and steam 2 minutes. Serve over hot pasta; top with grated Romano cheese.

Makes 4 to 6 servings

Favorite recipe from **Christopher Ranch of Gilroy**

Pesto Pasta

Pesto Pasta

Prep/Cook time: 20 minutes

- **1 cup packed fresh basil leaves**
- **1 (3-ounce) package KRAFT® 100% Shredded Parmesan Cheese or KRAFT® 100% Parmesan Cheese wedge, shredded, divided**
- **⅓ cup olive oil**
- **¼ cup pine nuts**
- **1 clove garlic, minced**
- **8 ounces uncooked radiatore pasta, hot cooked and drained**
- **1 cup pitted ripe olive halves**
- **1 cup chopped seeded tomatoes**

- Place basil, ½ cup cheese, oil, pine nuts and garlic in food processor container with steel blade attached; process until smooth.

- Toss together basil mixture, pasta, olives and tomatoes in large bowl. Sprinkle with remaining ¼ cup cheese.

Makes 4 servings

Variation: Substitute 8 ounces of your favorite pasta for the radiatore pasta.

Linguine with Oil and Garlic

10 cloves garlic, minced
½ cup FILIPPO BERIO® Extra-Virgin Flavorful Olive Oil, divided
¾ pound uncooked linguine
¼ teaspoon black pepper
¼ teaspoon salt, optional

1. Cook and stir garlic in 2 tablespoons olive oil in small saucepan over medium heat until lightly browned. Remove from heat; set aside.

2. Cook linguine according to package directions until tender. Do not overcook.

3. Drain pasta; return to pot. Toss with garlic and oil, remaining 6 tablespoons oil, pepper and salt.
Makes 4 servings

Vegetable Pasta with Cheese

Prep Time: 10 minutes
Cook Time: 15 minutes

1 package (12 ounces) uncooked mostaccioli
2 cups DOLE® Broccoli florettes
2 cups DOLE® Cauliflower florettes
1 cup sliced DOLE® Carrots
1 cup (4 ounces) shredded mozzarella cheese
1 cup (4 ounces) shredded Monterey Jack cheese
1 cup (4 ounces) shredded fontina cheese
⅓ cup grated Parmesan cheese, divided
3 tablespoons margarine, melted

• Cook pasta according to package directions; add vegetables during last 2 minutes of cooking. Drain.

• Gently toss pasta mixture in large bowl with shredded cheeses, 2½ tablespoons Parmesan cheese and margarine. Turn into large casserole dish.

• Sprinkle top with remaining Parmesan cheese.

• Bake in 450°F oven 5 minutes or until cheese melts.
Makes 6 servings

Tip: Cheeses may be shredded in food processor.

Vegetable Pasta with Cheese

Fettuccine with Sun-Dried Tomato Cream

Prep time: 30 minutes

2/3 cup sun-dried tomatoes (*not* packed in oil)
3 to 4 garlic cloves
1 (8-ounce) container PHILADELPHIA BRAND® Soft Cream Cheese
1/2 teaspoon dried oregano leaves, crushed
1/4 cup PARKAY® Margarine
1/4 cup sour cream
1 pound uncooked fettuccine, hot cooked and drained
1/4 cup olive oil
Salt and pepper
2 tablespoons chopped parsley

• Cover tomatoes with boiling water; let stand 10 minutes. Drain.

• Place tomatoes and garlic in covered food processor or blender container; process until coarsely chopped. Add cream cheese and oregano; process until well blended.

• Melt margarine in medium saucepan; stir in cream cheese mixture and sour cream. Cook until thoroughly heated.

• Toss hot fettuccine with oil in large bowl.

• Add cream cheese mixture. Season with salt and pepper to taste. Sprinkle with chopped parsley. Serve immediately.

Makes 8 to 10 servings

Italian Rice and Vegetables

5 tablespoons BUTTER FLAVOR CRISCO®, divided
1 cup uncooked long-grain rice
1/2 cup uncooked spaghetti pieces (1-inch long)
1/2 teaspoon salt
1/2 teaspoon Italian seasoning
1/8 teaspoon pepper
2 cups hot water
1 package (10 ounces) frozen chopped broccoli, thawed
1 cup sliced fresh mushrooms
3/4 cup quartered cherry tomatoes

In 2-quart saucepan, melt 3 tablespoons BUTTER FLAVOR CRISCO®. Add uncooked rice and spaghetti. Cook and stir over medium heat until rice and noodles are golden brown. Stir in salt, Italian seasoning, pepper and hot water. Heat to boiling. Reduce heat; cover and simmer about 15 minutes, or until water is absorbed. Set aside.

In large skillet, melt remaining 2 tablespoons BUTTER FLAVOR CRISCO®. Add broccoli, mushrooms and tomatoes. Cook and stir over medium heat until mushrooms are tender. Add rice mixture. Cook and stir until heated through.

Makes 6 servings

Fettuccine with Sun-Dried Tomato Cream

Southwestern Pasta Sauce

Spinach Tortellini with Roasted Red Peppers

2 packages (9 ounces each)
   fresh spinach tortellini
1 jar (7 ounces) roasted red
   peppers or pimientos,
   drained
2 tablespoons butter or
   olive oil
4 cloves garlic, minced
¼ cup chopped fresh basil *or*
   2 teaspoons dried basil,
   crushed
½ cup chopped walnuts,
   toasted
1 cup prepared HIDDEN VALLEY
   RANCH® Original Ranch
   Salad Dressing
   Additional fresh basil leaves,
   optional

Cook tortellini according to package directions; drain and set aside. Slice red peppers into strips; set aside. In large saucepan, melt butter; add garlic. Cook and stir about 2 minutes. Add red pepper strips, ¼ cup chopped basil and tortellini. Stir to coat; add walnuts. Stir in enough salad dressing so mixture is creamy and tortellini are coated. Garnish with additional fresh basil, if desired. Serve hot.

Makes 4 to 6 servings

Southwestern Pasta Sauce

¼ cup olive oil
2 medium onions, sliced
1 clove garlic, minced
1 can (28 to 29 ounces)
   tomatoes, undrained,
   coarsely chopped
2 to 3 tablespoons minced
   fresh cilantro
¾ teaspoon TABASCO® Pepper
   Sauce
¼ teaspoon salt
¼ teaspoon sugar
12 ounces uncooked angel hair
   pasta, hot cooked and
   drained
   Parmesan cheese, optional

Heat oil over medium heat in large, heavy non-aluminum saucepan. Stir in onions and garlic; cook and stir 10 to 12 minutes, stirring occasionally, until onions are tender. Add tomatoes with juice, cilantro, TABASCO® sauce, salt and sugar; bring to a boil. Reduce heat to low; simmer, uncovered, 30 minutes or until slightly thickened. Place hot cooked pasta on heated serving platter; top with sauce. Sprinkle with Parmesan cheese if desired.

Makes 4 servings

Pasta Primavera

- ⅓ cup chopped onion
- 3 tablespoons margarine or butter
- 3 tablespoons flour
- 1 cup water
- 2 medium carrots, pared and sliced
- 1 tablespoon WYLER'S® or STEERO® Chicken-Flavor Instant Bouillon
- ¾ teaspoon basil leaves
- 1 cup broccoli flowerets
- 1 cup sliced fresh mushrooms
- 1 cup sliced summer squash
- 1 cup BORDEN® or MEADOW GOLD® Half-and-Half
- ¼ teaspoon pepper
- ½ (1-pound) package CREAMETTE® Fettuccini, cooked according to package directions and drained
- Grated Parmesan cheese, optional

In large saucepan, cook onion in margarine until tender; stir in flour until smooth. Add water, carrots, bouillon and basil; bring to a boil. Reduce heat; cover and simmer 5 minutes. Add broccoli, mushrooms and squash; cook 5 minutes. Add half-and-half and pepper; cook and stir until slightly thickened. Serve over hot fettuccini. Garnish with cheese if desired. Refrigerate leftovers.

Makes 4 servings

Pasta Primavera

Pasta Antipasto

- ¾ cup **WISH-BONE® Italian Dressing**
- 2 green or red bell peppers, cut into strips
- ½ cup sliced celery
- 3 medium tomatoes, coarsely chopped
- 1 package (9 ounces) frozen artichoke hearts, partially thawed
- 1 cup sliced mushrooms
- 1 cup pitted ripe olives
- 1 can (2 ounces) drained anchovies, optional
- ½ pound uncooked ziti macaroni
- 8 ounces (2 cups) shredded mozzarella cheese

In medium skillet, heat Italian dressing. Cook and stir bell peppers and celery in Italian dressing until celery is crisp-tender. Add tomatoes, artichokes and mushrooms; cover and cook 15 minutes or until vegetables are tender. Add olives and anchovies; heat through.

Meanwhile, cook ziti according to package directions. Immediately toss with cheese and vegetable mixture.

Makes about 4 servings

Noodles Alfredo

- ½ pound uncooked wide egg noodles or fettuccine
- ¼ cup butter or margarine
- ½ cup half-and-half or light cream
- 1 cup (3 ounces) **SARGENTO® Fancy Shredded Parmesan Cheese**
- 1 tablespoon dried parsley flakes
- ¼ teaspoon salt
  Dash pepper

Cook noodles according to package directions; drain. Place in large serving bowl; keep warm.

Melt butter in 1-quart saucepan over low heat. Stir in half-and-half, Parmesan cheese, parsley, salt and pepper until thoroughly mixed and smooth. Pour warm sauce over hot noodles, stirring gently until noodles are well coated. *Makes 6 servings*

Pasta Amatriciana

- 8 slices uncooked bacon, coarsely chopped
- 1 large onion, thinly sliced
- 1 can (16 ounces) tomatoes in juice, undrained
- ½ teaspoon salt
- ¼ teaspoon crushed red pepper
  Pinch sugar
- 7 ounces **MUELLER'S® Pasta Swirls®**, hot cooked and drained
  Freshly ground black pepper

In large skillet, cook bacon over medium-high heat until crisp. Remove; set aside. Drain all but 3 tablespoons fat. Add onion to skillet. Reduce heat to medium; cook and stir 10 to 15 minutes or until golden. Add tomatoes with juice, crushing tomatoes with fork. Stir in salt, red pepper and sugar. Bring to a boil. Reduce heat to low; cover and simmer 10 minutes. Add bacon; blend well. Spoon over pasta in large bowl; toss to coat. Serve with black pepper. *Makes 4 servings*

Fresh Tomato Pasta Andrew

Fresh Tomato Pasta Andrew

- **1 pound fresh tomatoes, cut into wedges**
- **1 cup packed fresh basil leaves**
- **2 cloves garlic, chopped**
- **2 tablespoons olive oil**
- **8 ounces Camenzola cheese *or* 6 ounces ripe Brie plus two ounces Stilton cheese, each cut into small pieces**
- **Salt and white pepper to taste**
- **4 ounces uncooked angel hair pasta, vermicelli or other thin pasta, hot cooked and drained**
- **Grated Parmesan cheese**

Place tomatoes, basil, garlic and oil in covered food processor or blender; pulse on and off until ingredients are coarsely chopped, but not puréed. Combine tomato mixture and Camenzola cheese in large bowl. Season to taste with salt and white pepper. Add pasta; toss gently until cheese melts. Serve with Parmesan cheese. Garnish as desired.

Makes 2 main-dish or 4 side-dish servings

Favorite recipe from **California Tomato Advisory Board**

Al Fresco Pasta

Prep time: 5 minutes
Cook time: 10 minutes

**2 cups zucchini slices, cut in
    half**
2 tablespoons olive oil
2 cups chopped tomatoes
1 teaspoon italian seasoning
1 teaspoon garlic powder
**⅛ teaspoon ground red
    pepper**
½ cup chicken broth
**½ pound uncooked spaghetti,
    hot cooked and drained**
Parmesan cheese, optional

Cook and stir zucchini in hot oil in
large skillet over medium-high
heat about 5 minutes or until
tender. Add tomatoes, seasonings
and chicken broth. Reduce heat
to low; simmer, stirring frequently,
5 minutes or until sauce has
thickened slightly. Spoon sauce
over spaghetti in large bowl. If
desired, serve with Parmes
cheese. **Makes 4 servings**

Al Fresco Pasta

Microwave Marinara Sauce

2 cloves garlic, minced
½ cup chopped onion
2 tablespoons olive oil
**1¾ cups (14½-ounce can)
    CONTADINA® Whole Peeled
    Tomatoes, undrained,
    chopped**
**1 cup (8-ounce can)
    CONTADINA® Tomato
    Sauce**
½ teaspoon salt
**½ teaspoon dried basil,
    crushed**
**½ teaspoon dried oregano,
    crushed**
**Pasta (tortellini, ravioli,
    spaghetti, fusilli, linguine,
    twists, fettuccine, gnochi or
    small shells), hot cooked
    and drained**

In 2-quart microwave-safe dish,
microwave garlic and onion in oil
on HIGH (100%) power for 3
minutes, or until onion is
translucent. Stir in tomatoes with
juice, tomato sauce, salt, basil
and oregano. Microwave on
HIGH power for an additional 7 to
8 minutes. Toss with hot pasta in
large bowl.
Makes about 2 cups sauce

Stovetop Directions: In medium
saucepan, heat oil. Cook and stir
garlic and onion until onion is
translucent. Stir in tomatoes with
juice, tomato sauce, salt, basil
and oregano. Bring to a boil;
reduce heat. Simmer for 15
minutes, stirring occasionally. Toss
with hot pasta in large bowl.

Sweet Peppered Pasta

Sweet Peppered Pasta

    3 tablespoons MAZOLA®
      Corn Oil
 ½ cup finely chopped onion
 ½ cup minced red bell pepper
 ½ cup minced yellow bell
      pepper
    3 large cloves garlic, minced
 ⅓ cup water
    2 tablespoons chopped fresh
      basil
    1 chicken-flavor bouillon cube
 ¼ teaspoon crushed red
      pepper
    7 ounces MUELLER'S® Pasta
      Ruffles, hot cooked and
      drained
    Salad greens, optional

In large skillet, heat corn oil over
medium-high heat. Add onion,
red and yellow bell peppers and
garlic; cook and stir 4 minutes. Stir
in water, basil, bouillon cube, and
crushed red pepper. Bring to a
boil, stirring occasionally. Reduce
heat to low; simmer 4 minutes.
Spoon over pasta in large bowl;
toss to coat well. Serve on
assorted salad greens if desired.

Makes 6 servings

Linguine with Fresh Tomato Basil Sauce

    1 cup chopped onion
    3 cloves garlic, minced
 ¼ teaspoon ground black
      pepper
    2 tablespoons FLEISCHMANN'S®
      Margarine
    2 cups sliced mushrooms
    3 large tomatoes, peeled,
      seeded and chopped
    1 tablespoon dried basil
      leaves, crushed, *or* ¼ cup
      chopped fresh basil leaves
    1 teaspoon sugar
  12 ounces uncooked linguine,
      cooked according to
      package directions in
      unsalted water and
      drained

In large skillet, over medium-high
heat, cook and stir onion, garlic
and pepper in margarine until
onion is tender, about 3 minutes.
Add mushrooms; cook for 5
minutes. Add tomatoes, basil and
sugar; heat to a boil. Reduce
heat to low; simmer, uncovered,
15 to 20 minutes. Serve over
linguine.   *Makes 6 servings*

Zesty Artichoke Basil Sauce

¾ cup (6-ounce jar) marinated artichoke hearts, drained and marinade reserved
1 cup slivered onion
1 large clove garlic, minced
1¾ cups (14½-ounce can) CONTADINA® Whole Peeled Tomatoes, undrained
⅔ cup (6-ounce can) CONTADINA® Tomato Paste
1 cup water
2 tablespoons chopped fresh basil
½ teaspoon salt

In 2½-quart saucepan, heat reserved artichoke marinade. Cook and stir onion and garlic in marinade for 2 to 3 minutes or until tender. Chop artichoke hearts; add to onion mixture with tomatoes and juice, tomato paste, water, basil and salt. Break up tomatoes. Bring to a boil; reduce heat to low. Simmer, uncovered, 15 to 20 minutes.

Makes 4 cups sauce

Savory Caper and Olive Sauce: Eliminate marinated artichoke hearts and basil. In 2½-quart saucepan, heat 2 tablespoons olive oil. Cook and stir onion and garlic for 2 to 3 minutes or until tender. Add ¾ cup sliced and quartered zucchini, tomatoes and juice, tomato paste, water, salt, ½ cup (2¼-ounce can) drained, sliced ripe olives and 2 tablespoons drained capers. Proceed as directed above.

Zesty Artichoke Basil Sauce

ACKNOWLEDGMENTS

*The publishers would like to thank the companies and organizations
listed below for the use of their recipes in this publication.*

Armour Swift-Eckrich
Best Foods, a Division of CPC
    International Inc.
Borden Kitchens, Borden, Inc.
California Apricot Advisory Board
California Poultry Industry
    Federation
California Tomato Advisory Board
Canned Food Information
    Council
Christopher Ranch of Gilroy
Contadina Foods, Inc., Nestlé
    Food Company
The Creamette Company
Del Monte Corporation
Dole Food Company
Filippo Berio Olive Oil
Heinz U.S.A.
Hunt-Wesson, Inc.
The HVR Company
Kraft General Foods, Inc.
Thomas J. Lipton Co.

McIlhenny Company
Nabisco Foods Group
National Live Stock and Meat
    Board
National Pasta Association
New Jersey Department of
    Agriculture
Norseland Foods, Inc.
North Dakota Beef Commission
North Dakota Dairy Promotion
    Commission
North Dakota Wheat Commission
Oscar Mayer Foods Corporation
Pace Foods, Inc.
The Procter & Gamble
    Company, Inc.
Reckitt & Colman Inc.
Sargento Cheese Company, Inc.
Shade Pasta, Inc.
StarKist Seafood Company
Virginia Marine Products Board
Walnut Marketing Board

PHOTO CREDITS

*The publishers would like to thank the companies and organizations
listed below for the use of their photographs in this publication.*

Armour Swift-Eckrich
Best Foods, a Division of CPC
    International Inc.
Borden Kitchens, Borden, Inc.
California Apricot Advisory Board
California Poultry Industry
    Federation
California Tomato Advisory Board
Canned Food Information
    Council
Contadina Foods, Inc., Nestlé
    Food Company
Del Monte Corporation
Dole Food Company
Hunt-Wesson, Inc.
The HVR Company
Kraft General Foods, Inc.
Thomas J. Lipton Co.

McIlhenny Company
Nabisco Foods Group
National Live Stock and Meat
    Board
National Pasta Association
New Jersey Department of
    Agriculture
North Dakota Beef Commission
North Dakota Dairy Promotion
    Commission
North Dakota Wheat Commission
Pace Foods, Inc.
Reckitt & Colman Inc.
Sargento Cheese Company, Inc.
StarKist Seafood Company
Virginia Marine Products Board
Walnut Marketing Board

INDEX